Practical Policing Skills
for Student Officers

Practical Policing Skills
for Student Officers

Second Edition

Editor
SUE MADSEN

Contributors
DAVID CROW
AMANDA FORM
GARY FRASER
TREFOR GILES

Series Editor
GARY WYNN

LawMatters
PUBLISHING

Published by Law Matters Publishing
33 Southernhay East
Exeter EX1 1NX
Tel: 01392 215577

First published in 2006
This second edition published in 2007

British Library Cataloguing-in-Publication Data

A catalogue record for this book is available from the British Library.

ISBN 978 1 84641 052 9

Typeset by Pantek Arts Ltd, Maidstone, Kent

Printed by Cromwell Press Ltd, Trowbridge, Wiltshire

Contents

Introduction   vii

1   Role of the Student Police Officer   1

2   Skills and Assessment   6

3   Driving Documents   18

4   Youth Nuisance/Disorder   43

5   Missing Persons   62

6   Shoplifting   79

7   Burglary   102

8   Domestic Violence   116

Appendix 1   139

Appendix 2   155

Index   161

Introduction

This book will help student police officers transfer the knowledge and skills obtained during their initial training into the workplace using practical policing scenarios. It will be a useful manual for the newly appointed student police officer (SO) as well as a helpful guidance document for those already in post. Those wishing to apply for the role of SO may also find the book useful as preparation material for the assessment process.

The role of the police constable in the modern police service is both challenging and rewarding. It is the allure of not knowing what a tour of duty may bring that attracts many people to the role. A tour of duty may require a constable to deal with a variety of incidents, ranging from dealing with a lost child to being first on the scene at a serious incident such as a murder. Regardless of the incident, student officers are provided with extensive training designed to equip them with the skills and knowledge to deal with a range of incidents.

This book accompanies and enhances those skills and knowledge, the chapters cover everyday incidents that a constable would expect to encounter. The book is structured into three main sections:

Section 1

Chapter 1 – Explanation of the role of the SO, the powers allocated to the role and the competencies contained within the Role Profile.

Section 2

Chapter 2 – Explanation of the skills and abilities required by a SO, including the National Occupational Standards allocated to the role and how they will be used in workplace assessment.

Section 3

Chapters 3–8

These are the scenario-based chapters, each one dealing in a structured way with a different policing issue. The structure for each chapter is as follows:

Identify the problem, Research the problem, Develop a plan, Implement the plan, Action taken.

The scenarios are chosen to mirror the problems that will be encountered regularly within the workplace by a SO and are as follows:

- **Driving documents** – Commonplace minor traffic-related issues such as obstruction and parking. Responding to ongoing traffic-related problems, the checks that are required, powers that apply regarding production of documentation and how to complete the relevant documentation and processes involved.

- **Youth nuisance (anti-social behaviour)** – The current problem of youth nuisance and disorder, the effect that it can have on communities and how to implement a problem-orientated policing plan.

- **Missing persons** – Preparing, attending and documenting missing person enquiries, how to gather evidence, conduct and finalise an investigation, including witness interviews and questioning.

- **Shoplifting (theft)** – Attending a report of shoplifting, dealing with suspect, property, witnesses and the investigation. Including custody procedures and suspect interviews.

- **Burglary** – Initial action on attending a burglary scene, dealing with and preserving forensic evidence, crime scene management, crime prevention and how to conduct an investigation.

- **Domestic violence** – Attending an initial report, personal safety, victim care and support, powers to deal with offences and other agencies that may assist. Custody procedures, how to gather evidence, document it and conduct an investigation.

How to make the most of the scenarios

Each chapter provides you with an introduction to the scenario that puts it into the policing context. They reflect an actual incident; details of the incident are then outlined and provide you with the information you need to progress through the scenario. Just as in an actual incident, the scenario may change and new dilemmas may be encountered that require you to make a decision. The chapters reflect this changing environment. Throughout the scenario you are asked a series of pertinent questions in relation to the scenario and the actions you would consider taking. Each question is then answered. This process is repeated throughout the scenario. The questions are formulated to encourage the reader to use a structured, logical and problem-solving thought process. The questions used are:

- What do you know?

- What do you need to know?

◆ How are you going to find that out?

◆ What next?

This process can be transferred into the workplace and will provide a good basis for dealing with issues when performing the role of SO on a day-to-day basis. At times there may be additional questions asked to gain maximum benefit from the scenario.

At the end of each scenario a flowchart has been included to provide an at-a-glance guide to dealing with the given scenarios. The flowchart follows the same structure as the scenario and gives bullet-point advice regarding options or avenues that can be taken by the SO attending or dealing with the specific issue.

Methods of assessment

The initial page of each scenario outlines the National Occupational Standards and Role Profile areas that could be claimed for workplace assessment by the SO. This is an overall view for the whole scenario.

Throughout the scenario this process is repeated periodically. This breaks down the scenarios and highlights where, after each relevant section, the specific standards or areas may have been achieved. This will enable the reader to identify what information would need to be included in the relevant documentation to be submitted to an assessor/supervisor in order to claim the required competencies.

The assessment methods and documentation that may be used to claim evidence of competence by the SO are outlined and explained at the end of each chapter.

Chapter 1
Role of the Student Police Officer

Introduction

In order to gain the maximum benefit from this book it is important that you first and foremost understand what the Role Profile and job requirements of the student police officer (SO) are. This chapter will explain the SO Role Profile in simple terms and outline the job requirements for the SO within the police service. You will also gain a greater understanding of what the SO is expected to achieve within the two-year probationary period and what the criteria that they are assessed against consists of.

This chapter may also be useful to those hoping to apply to become a student police officer as the current application and assessment processes are based upon the role profile/competencies explained during this chapter.

The role

The government has recently implemented the Initial Police Learning and Development Programme (IPLDP) to be adopted by all forces. This is a national training and assessment programme for student officers that they will follow for the duration of their two-year probationary period. The SO will not be confirmed in their appointment as a police constable until they have successfully completed the programme. We will explore the IPLDP in more detail in Chapter 2.

The SO will follow a specified structure for the two-year period that will differ slightly from force to force but all will have the same underlying principles to guide the student through a process of training and assessment. The following is a guide to the process which has been broken down into phases to highlight the route that the student officer will follow.

Phase 1
Induction – An induction phase will take place normally within the force to which the person has been recruited or at a designated training establishment.

Phase 2

Initial training – This phase is to provide the student with the underpinning knowledge, understanding and skills to deal with day-to-day policing activities. It will normally be classroom based and will cover areas such as legislation, procedures, policies, powers and some skills in relation to personal safety and first aid training. Although this phase may be classroom based it is possible that it could also include role-plays, examinations and some form of community involvement. Dependent on the individual force this training may be within a police training centre or within an external educational establishment such as a college or university.

Phase 3

Accompanied Patrol/Tutelage – At this point the student will be placed with a competent police officer (tutor constable) who will work with them in an operational policing environment, where they will deal with day-to-day policing incidents. This is the stage where the student will be expected to put into practice the learning from the previous phase. The duration of this phase may vary from force to force, as will the structure. For example, some students will complete perhaps a full ten-week period with a tutor while others may have this split and complete five weeks, then return for some further classroom training to then complete a further five weeks tutelage at a later date.

Whilst on this phase the students will be assessed against set criteria to determine whether or not they are suitable for independent patrol. The criteria used are called Police Action Checklists (PACs) and it will be the responsibility of the tutor constable to assess the student. We will explore the PACs further in Chapter 2.

Phase 4

Independent patrol – This consists of the student being placed into the workplace as part of a regular policing team in an operational environment. They will be patrolling unaccompanied and will be expected to deal with day-to-day policing incidents as they occur.

It is generally at this point that the student will be gathering the majority of the evidence that they will use to claim competence against the 22 National Occupational Standards (NOS). We will explore the NOS further in Chapter 2.

Throughout this stage the student will receive a minimum of 30 hours specified training which is designed to broaden their skills, knowledge and understanding. This has been termed 'protected learning' and it can be delivered in a variety of ways, which will be dependent on the individual force. These may include being in a training centre, other educational establishment or within a policing area/division. It is stipulated that the training time must be 'protected' and not part of the student's operational duties. The subject matter that is covered on this training normally consists of more advanced topics that were not covered in the initial training phase, such as sexual offences, critical incidents, etc.

Phase 5

Confirmation of appointment – When the student has completed two years' service and been assessed as competent in the relevant areas they will have their appointment as a police constable confirmed.

National Occupational Standards

The National Occupational Standards (NOS) form the basis of the SO job description; the Role Profile, and training and assessment are all developed from these standards. The NOS for the role are monitored and updated by an organisation named Skills for Justice (Skills for Justice are the dedicated sector skills council and standards body for the justice sector). They work alongside justice sector organisations and identify the skills, priorities and actions required for workplace development.

There are 22 NOS that have been identified for the role of SO. We will continue to explore the NOS in more detail in Chapter 2.

Role Profile

Within the police service a competency framework known as the Integrated Competency Framework (ICF) has been introduced. This framework outlines the required competencies for the individual roles and has ensured a common standard for individual role profiles throughout the service. It can be used to plan training needs, compile job descriptions, assist recruitment, and monitor staff to improve performance.

A Role Profile will form the basis of any performance reviews or appraisals carried out on a role holder. The competencies relevant to the Role Profile ensure the person or task is assessed against a set of agreed standards. Role competencies therefore help to enforce a structured, transparent and objective assessment process which can be used by supervisors, managers or the post holders themselves to gather evidence of performance. A Role Profile will also state the relevant National Occupational Standards (NOS) upon which the profile has been formulated.

Role Profiles may differ slightly between forces simply because the job require-ments vary in each policing area. Nevertheless, the core elements of the SO Role Profile (generic skills) are the same across the police service.

Skills for Justice have produced a Role Profile for the SO; this is the recom-mended national Role Profile and will therefore be used as a benchmark for this book (see **Appendix 1**). Please note that the profile used in the book is mapped only to the 22 NOS used for student officer assessment. Any additional Role Profile information you require can be requested from your local police force and dealt with using the same principles you will see outlined within the book.

Structure of a Role Profile

A Role Profile is made up of core responsibilities, activities and behaviours. We will explore each in turn.

- ◆ **Core responsibilities**
  As the title suggests, these are the areas of responsibility that are central to the Role Profile; examples of these for the SO role are custody and prosecu-tion and investigation.

- ◆ **Activities**
  These are the specific tasks/activities that a person is expected to perform in their role; they are explained in a Role Profile in the form of a description of what effective performance should be. These activities are grouped together under the relevant core responsibility area and each activity is allocated an activity number and referenced to the relevant NOS.

- ◆ **Behaviours**
  The areas/standards of behaviour expected of a person carrying out a role are separated into behaviour areas and behaviour descriptions. The areas are the titles and overall definitions, whereas the descriptions outline what is expected from the role holder. Behaviours are not to be dealt with in isola-tion, as the standard of behaviour can easily affect the activities. To achieve competence in a role three different levels of behaviour need to be attained, usually at levels A, B or C (respect for race and diversity behaviour is always a level A). Examples of behaviours for the role of SO are working with others and achieving results.

Throughout the practical scenario chapters of this book you will be reminded of the appropriate SO role behaviours/activities in one of two ways. First of all, at the very beginning of each chapter you will find a table listing the National Occupational Standards and the activities/behaviours relevant to the scenario as a whole. Secondly, at regular points during the scenario there are a series of shaded boxes which remind you of the SO activities/behaviours appropriate to particular sections of the scenario. The activities/behaviours will be indicated in the shaded boxes by the following symbol: ❖

Please see **Appendix 1** for a detailed example of a Role Profile.

Chapter 2
Skills and Assessment

Introduction

In the previous chapter we explored the Integrated Competency Framework (ICF) and the contents of a Role Profile for a SO. In this chapter we will examine the specific skills and abilities required in order to achieve competence in the role and how this is underpinned by the National Occupational Standards (NOS). We will also look at how the SO may be continually monitored and assessed against the NOS during the training and development period and within the workplace.

Training and development

The recently introduced Initial Police Learning and Development Programme (IPLDP) is the national training programme for SO, and is designed to be developed and delivered on a local level to accommodate the needs of individual forces. It is intended to allow the officers to embark on a process of development for the rest of their career. Although the programme has been 'localised', the Home Office together with members of the police service have established the 'IPLDP central authority' that will provide guidance and direction to forces and ensure that minimum standards are met locally and nationally.

When the IPLDP was first introduced, individual forces made the choice of how they would implement the guidelines set by the government. Some forces decided their student officers should complete a 'foundation degree in policing'. This training is normally provided by an external training provider such as a university and includes a form of workplace/workplace-related assessment. Others decided their students should be trained within police establishments and then assessed in the workplace against the NOS to achieve a National Vocational Qualification (NVQ) in policing. All training provided will be mapped against the NOS to ensure its relevance to the role and the preparation of the individual for the workplace.

Most recently the IPLDP central authority has given a directive that the national qualification for student officers will comprise of all 22 NOS and that NVQ level 3 and NVQ level 4 in policing must be achieved. (There are 11 NOS in the level 3 and 11 NOS in the level 4.) The central authority intended to ensure that all forces had the required mechanisms in place so that the national qualification would be available from April 2007. Thus the achievement of NVQ 3 and 4 in policing is mandatory for all student officers. Therefore, this book will provide the reader with guidance of how to recognise when the relevant evidence may have been achieved and how this could be produced for assessment to achieve the relevant NOS and in turn the NVQ.

Work-based assessment

Assessing competence in a job using the NOS has been used by many different sectors in the past. Work-based assessment is now commonly used within the police service in a variety of areas, including criminal investigation training (ICIDP) and sergeant/inspector promotion processes. The SO is no exception to this and as outlined previously, the role holder will be assessed within the workplace.

Whilst in the accompanied patrol (tutelage) phase the SO will be assessed against a set of criteria called the Policing Action Checklists (PACs). These are the triggers for independent patrol for the student and they also inform managers of what a student officer can do at the point of independent patrol without the need for immediate direct supervision. PACs, as the name suggests, are a list of policing actions/tasks that are to be achieved. They are not a definitive statement of competence and only indicate that the student can perform certain tasks, not that they are competent at the task. PACs are based on NOS but are a means of checking the ability of a student officer at a particular time, as opposed to competence in the role that is assessed against the actual NOS. The tutor constable will carry out the assessment of the PACs. Dependent on the individual force, students will need to complete all or a given percentage of the PACs before they can progress to independent patrol.

The student officer will then move on to assessment against the NOS.

National Occupational Standards

National Occupational Standards (NOS) outline the key competencies and knowledge necessary for certain job roles. When coupled with an assessment strategy, they provide clear guidelines for the assessment of competence in a specific job role against nationally agreed standards of performance. NOS are widely used to provide benchmarks of best practice across the United Kingdom.

They can also form a qualification for the relevant role holder, including a National Vocational Qualification (NVQ). The NOS are particularly important to the police service as they offer a set of competency guidelines that are flexible enough to meet the specific needs of all forces. As previously outlined for the SO, there have been 22 NOS identified and the qualification to be obtained from these will be the NVQ levels 3 and 4 in policing.

Structure of National Occupational Standards

The NOS are grouped together by Skills for Justice into particular occupational areas/sectors; for policing roles they are taken from the policing and law enforcement sector. The NOS are broken down into individual units. These units describe competent performance and are made up of a number of individual parts which combine to fulfil the required outcomes and role competencies. These parts are as follows.

◆ **Unit summary**
This describes what the unit is about and how it fits into the workplace. It may outline the type of incidents or activities to which the unit applies. Each unit is given a number, for example 1A1.

◆ **Elements**
Units are divided into elements. A unit can be comprised of anything between one and five individual elements. An element consists of performance criteria and range. Each element is given a number, for example 1A1.1, 1A1.2.

◆ **Performance criteria**
The element will contain a list of performance criteria. These clearly describe the performance required by the role holder to achieve competence. (They should not be treated as a list of tasks.)

◆ **Range**
Within the performance criteria certain areas are highlighted to suggest a range of possible applications. When a range is given, this means candidates will need to demonstrate competence within the performance criteria and also across the specified range.

◆ **Knowledge and understanding**
This is what a role holder will need to know and understand in order to perform competently within the unit. This is the basic underpinning knowledge and understanding of policies, procedures, facts, opinions, theories, etc. This is the final part of a unit and will cover the whole unit.

+ **Evidence requirements**

    These outline the evidence required by the role holder in order to achieve competency in the unit. They may state, for example, that the performance criteria needs to be displayed on a given number of separate occasions or that the range is required a specific number of times.

National Occupational Standards for Student Police Officers

The following list outlines the 22 standards in which competence is required for student police officers, this is broken down into the NVQ level 3 and 4 units.

NVQ Policing Level 3 units

1A1 – Use police actions in a fair and justified way

This focuses on the use of officer actions and applies across the use of all police powers. Police actions must be used proportionately and fairly and be legitimate, necessary and lawful within the circumstances.

+ This could include stop/search/detention/issue of tickets or in fact any action taken by an officer.

1A4 – Foster people's equality, diversity and rights

The acknowledgement of equality and diversity, including a person's rights and responsibilities is the principal aim of this particular occupational standard. It also includes the need for confidentiality, particularly when handling sensitive information. It is expected the officer will be proactive against discrimination and will try to diffuse any specific tensions arising in an individual or among different people. The term 'people' includes individuals, families, groups, communities and organisations, or anyone else you may come into contact with.

+ This could include any situations dealt with that may include an element of the following: race/ethnicity, religion/faith, sexual orientation, social status, poverty, physical/learning disability, mental health, age gender/sex, migrants, asylum seekers, travellers, non-English-speaking groups, single parents, unemployed, students, mixed heritage, family status, political belief, etc.

    (This list is not exhaustive but gives an idea of the scope of this unit which can be evidenced within all areas of day-to-day duties)

2C1 – Provide an initial police response to incidents

This unit is about providing an initial response to incidents that may be encountered during duties. These may include domestic violence, critical incidents, road traffic incidents, public order, allegations of crime, non-crime incidents, and racist/hate crime incidents.

◆ Gathering information on the incidents can evidence this, e.g. history, dangers, witness details, etc. Then use that information to establish the nature of the incident and plan your actions accordingly; this process may happen quickly whilst on route to an incident or whilst dealing with it at the time. Health and safety needs to be considered when responding to incidents.

2C3 – Arrest, detain or report individuals

This unit is about conducting arrests, detentions and reporting procedures.

◆ To achieve this the officer will need to be able to conduct their actions legally in a balanced and proportionate manner, considering the impact of their actions on others. The correct techniques are to be used and any contingencies that arise are to be dealt with.

2C4 – Minimise and deal with aggressive and abusive behaviour

This unit is about acting in a way that does not provoke aggressive or abusive behaviour. It also covers defusing situations and protecting yourself when dealing with people who are or may become aggressive and abusive by breaking away from the situation. There is no requirement in this unit to use physical force.

◆ This can be evidenced when in this type of situation by showing respect for people, their property and their rights. Identifying and minimising any actions or words that may trigger abusive/aggressive behaviour. Take constructive action to defuse situations. Act in a way that is calm and reassuring. Physically break away, if necessary, from a threatening situation in a safe and effective manner.

2H1 – Interview victims and witnesses

This unit is about interviewing victims and witnesses as part of an investigation. It includes interviews at police premises and those held elsewhere.

◆ To evidence this the officer will need to plan and prepare for the interview and develop an interview strategy. Assess the interviewee's fitness for interview, set up the appropriate location and conduct the interview in accordance with legislation, policy and guidelines. Appropriate interview techniques and communication skills must be used and the interview must be evaluated and any necessary further actions taken in relation to the investigation and any suspects involved, e.g. charge, bail or release.

2I1 – Search individuals

This unit is about searching individuals for items suspected as being evidence of an offence or for the prevention of harm to self or others. The officer must first ensure that they have the grounds and legal authority to carry out the search.

- This can be achieved by identifying and dealing with any potential risks present (e.g. weapons, risk of violence being used, sharps, hazardous substances or warning signs). The search must be conducted in a legal, ethical manner using approved techniques. Any evidence found is to be seized, packaged and stored correctly maintaining integrity and continuity. The search results need to be communicated to the individual and other relevant persons and any document required must be completed in the correct manner.

2K2 – Present detained persons to custody

This unit is about presenting detained persons for the custody process. This covers people who have been arrested or otherwise deprived of their liberty. The officer will retain responsibility for the person until they are formally handed over to custody.

- To achieve competence in this the officer will have to explain the legality and grounds for detention to the relevant officer and provide them with any special conditions that may apply, e.g. vulnerable, segregation required. Any loss, damage or contamination of evidence must be minimised and where authorised a search of the person should be made. Where possible the identity of the person is to be verified and other background and previous history checks should be carried out.

4C1 – Develop one's own knowledge and practice

This unit is about the development of your own knowledge and practice. It involves reflecting on and evaluating your own interests, priorities and effectiveness.

- To achieve this the officer needs to reflect on the effectiveness of the outcomes and processes of their practices and learn from this. The learning may come from reflecting on your own practices or that of others and any new knowledge should be incorporated into your practice.

4G2 – Ensure your own actions reduce the risks to health and safety

This unit is about having an appreciation of significant risks in the workplace and knowing how to identify and deal with them. To gain competency a person must ensure that their own actions do not create any risks, they do not ignore significant risks within the workplace and take sensible action to put things right, e.g. reporting situations that could pose a risk or danger or seeking advice from the appropriate person.

- ◆ Reporting incidents to the responsible person, taking action to avoid/minimise risks or hazards and carrying out tasks safely in accordance with instructions and workplace requirements can evidence this. This evidence is likely to occur within day-to-day duties.

4G4 – Administer first aid

This is about the application of first aid in emergency situations. It covers the ability to respond promptly and appropriately to a range of situations and incidents, in order to preserve life and protect casualties until specialist aid is available.

- ◆ This can be evidenced by completion of a recognised first aid award or by actual first aid applied in day-to-day situations. Due to the nature of the role of a police officer it is unlikely that all of the evidence will be achieved using real situations; therefore simulations or role-plays may be used. These are normally incorporated into training for a recognised award.

NVQ Policing Level 4 units

1A2 – Communicate effectively with members of communities

This is about standards of communication when an officer has direct contact with members of the public.

- ◆ It can be achieved by developing and maintaining effective channels of communication, and respecting the culture, race/ethnicity of others. Communities are classed as neighbourhoods, communities of interest (such as business communities), and communities of identity (such as older people, minority ethnic groups, young people, lesbians, gay men, asylum seekers and travellers).

1B9 – Provide initial support to individuals affected by offending or anti-social behaviour and assess their needs for support

This looks at the initial contact and support an officer might give to individuals who have been affected by offending or anti-social behaviour. Support can be dependent on the needs and wishes of the individual and can be practical or emotional. This could simply involve listening to and reassuring the individual or arranging other support over a period of time. This may include court cases, those severely affected by their experience or those that are vulnerable. The individual may need to be assessed and any further support that they or their family may need agreed and discussed taking into account the wishes of the individual and the available resources. Sometimes you may need to balance the rights of the individual with any possible risks of harm to them or to others. It may also be necessary to seek advice and support from colleagues or specialists, especially if the individual is a child, in which instance parental responsibility should be sought. The term 'individual' can refer to the person to whom you are providing support, a victim/survivor of offending or anti-social behaviour, or the family and friends of a victim, especially in the case of bereaved families.

- This could include any situations dealt with that involve victims/witnesses or others involved that are affected by offending or anti-social behaviour. This could range from minor crime/disorder to more serious offences or road traffic incidents/collisions.

2A1 – Gather and submit information that has the potential to support policing objectives

This is about gathering information that has the potential to become intelligence and is therefore likely to assist with and support policing objectives. This unit works in accordance with the National Intelligence Model (NIM).

- To achieve this, information must be identified from a variety of situations and sources (human and technical) that has the potential to become intelligence. The role holder will need to conduct an initial assessment and grading of that information. The correct submission of intelligence reports from a variety of different sources in relation to different areas/incidents will help towards becoming competent in this unit.

2C2 – Prepare for, and participate in, planned policing operations

This unit is about taking part in planned policing operations and applies to all types of pre-planned operations, e.g. public order, sporting events, Royal visits, co-ordinated structured searches or firearms operations.

- The post holder will need to prepare themselves for the operations, be clear about their role and responsibilities, obtain the right equipment and complete the relevant documentation. They will also need to actually participate in the operations, carry out role and responsibilities as per the briefing, use the authorised equipment correctly and co-ordinate their actions with others involved in the operation.

2G2 – Conduct investigations

This unit is about conducting investigations at a general policing level.

- To achieve this the officer must gather and assess the available information and intelligence, conduct a risk assessment, identify and preserve the initial scene(s) and identify and deal with evidence. Initial enquiries should be developed and victims or witnesses dealt with appropriately. All relevant people should be regularly updated/briefed regarding the status of the investigation.

(This unit is applicable to all types of investigation, e.g. criminal, road traffic collisions and missing persons.)

2G4 – Finalise investigations

This unit is about ensuring that prior to completing/finalising an investigation all available evidence has been correctly compiled and submitted.

- Ensuring that victims and witnesses have been contacted and kept up to date with case progress can evidence this, as well as fully investigating any additional information in relation to the investigation, and liaising with the prosecuting authority. An officer must respond to any requests for further action and attend any pre-trial hearings as required.

(This unit is applicable to all types of investigation, e.g. criminal, road traffic collisions and missing persons.)

2H2 – Interview suspects

This unit is about interviewing suspects as part of an investigation, for all types of offence, and includes suspects under arrest and suspects not under arrest. Interviews conducted within police premises or elsewhere are covered in the unit.

- To achieve this the officer must plan and prepare for interview, develop an interview strategy, assess the suspect's fitness for interview and set up an appropriate location. The interview must be conducted using appropriate techniques and within the relevant legislation, policy and guidelines. It will also be expected for the officer to evaluate the interview and take any necessary further action, e.g. charge, bail or release suspect.

2I2 – Search vehicles, premises and land

This unit is about searches of vehicles, premises and land; land could include a garden, grass verge, yard, etc.

- To evidence this the search must be conducted in a legal and ethical way using approved search methods. The officer will need to ensure that they have the grounds and legal authority to carry out the search. Any evidence found will need to be seized, packaged and stored in the correct manner to ensure integrity and continuity and the correct documentation completed.

2J1 – Prepare and submit case files

This unit is about the preparation and submission of case files. These include overnight files, abbreviated (expedited) or full files. They could relate to prosecutions, road collisions, etc.

♦ To achieve this the officer will need to establish the status of the investigation, distinguish between different types of case materials and identify sensitive and non-sensitive material. Files will need to be submitted to internal departments and/or prosecuting authorities. All relevant documentation must have been completed correctly and any requests for further actions must be responded to.

2K1 – Escort detained persons

This unit focuses on the safe and secure escort of detained persons. Detained persons could be arrested or otherwise deprived of their liberty, they could be escorted from the point of detention into custody or from one secure environment to another. The escorting will be on foot and by vehicle. (Could entail escorting a person on foot to a vehicle.)

♦ Obtaining all relevant information regarding the detained person from the appropriate source, dealing with the detained person appropriately according to the risk that they pose, their level of compliance and vulnerability can evidence this. Detained persons must be escorted to the appropriate location. The officer will comply with any warrants or injunctions in existence and take responsibility for any evidence or personal property being transported with the detained person.

2J2 – Present evidence in court and at other hearings

This unit is about preparing and presenting evidence to courts and other hearings.

♦ This can be evidenced by correctly dealing with a criminal court warning or requests from other hearings such as coroner's court, criminal injury compensation agencies or civil court. A person must be fully prepared for the court/hearing in possession of all exhibits, notes and materials in advance and liaise with relevant parties. Then present evidence in various capacities, such as, officer in a case, arresting officer or witness in an effective manner, complying with the relevant rules and procedures.

Assessment documentation

The documentation used will be dependent on the method of training/development chosen by the individual force, e.g. NVQ, foundation degree. All documentation will be collected and placed into a portfolio of evidence. The name of this portfolio may differ from force to force; however, the nationally recommended document is the 'student officer learning assessment portfolio' (SOLAP); this is the document we will refer to throughout this book.

The student officer will need to produce/provide evidence from their workplace achievements to an assessor, this evidence can be from a variety of different sources. Examples of the type of evidence that could be used are as follows.

Witness testimonies/statements

These consist of obtaining a written or recorded testimony from a witness regarding what they have seen or heard you do. They will need to include full contact details of the witness, what their relationship is to the student and what their level of competence in the role is.

Personal statements

This will be a written or recorded statement from the student in relation to what they have done to achieve competence. These statements should include details of any supporting evidence such as paperwork completed, procedures conducted or other persons present at the time.

Product evidence

This will be an actual product that is given to the assessor to achieve competence; examples of this may be a case file or first aid certificate.

Observation

This will consist of a report being compiled by an assessor who has observed first hand your actions.

Questions

Evidence of competence may be gained by the student answering questions set by an assessor. A record must be made of the questions asked and answers produced in written or recorded format.

Professional discussion

An assessor can hold a discussion with the student that will be aimed at exploring certain areas to attain competence; this can be written or recorded.

It must be noted that where evidence is produced to an assessor that has not been observed first hand by an assessor, they will check the evidence and validate that the evidence is authentic, sufficient, valid and current before they award any competence.

There are other methods of assessment that may be used, such as examinations, simulations, etc. However, the methods outlined above will be the most likely to be used within workplace assessment of the policing NOS.

Throughout the practical scenario chapters of this book links will be made to the areas where, during the day-to-day duties of a SO, the NOS can be achieved and used as evidence of performance in a portfolio. There will also be suggestions regarding how the evidence could be presented/documented for assessment and the method of assessment used. These will be indicated by the portfolio symbol 🗁

To assist in the navigation of the book in relation to the NOS the following matrix will show at a glance the NOS that are covered in each chapter.

NOS	Chapters					
	3	4	5	6	7	8
Level 3						
1A1	•	•	•	•	•	•
1A4	•	•	•	•	•	•
2C1	•	•	•	•	•	•
2C3	•	•		•	•	•
2C4		•				•
2H1			•	•	•	
2I1		•		•	•	•
2K2		•		•	•	•
4C1	•	•	•	•	•	•
4G2	•	•		•	•	•
4G4						•
Level 4						
1A2	•	•				
1B9		•			•	•
2A1	•	•	•	•	•	•
2C2						
2G2			•	•	•	•
2G4			•	•	•	
2H2				•	•	
2I2			•	•	•	
2J1	•	•	•	•	•	•
2J2						
2K1		•		•	•	•

Chapter 3
Driving Documents

This chapter covers criteria within the following units of the National Occupational Standards for student police officers:

Level 3

1A1 – Use police actions in a fair and justified way.
1A4 – Foster people's equality, diversity and rights.
4G2 – Ensure your own actions reduce the risks to health and safety.
2C1 – Provide an initial police response to incidents.
2C3 – Arrest, detain or report individuals.
4C1 – Develop one's own knowledge and practice.

Level 4

2A1 – Gather and submit information that has the potential to support policing objectives.
1A2 – Communicate effectively with members of communities.
2J1 – Prepare and submit case files.

It is likely that the following activities and behaviours from the student officer Role Profile will also be evidenced.

Activities:

112 – Conduct patrol.
141 – Promote equality, diversity and human rights in working practice.
101 – Provide an initial response to incidents.
36 – Conduct lawful arrest and process procedures.
42 – Prepare and submit case files.
217 – Maintain standards of professional practice.
127 – Provide an effective response recognising the needs of all communities.
57 – Use information/intelligence to support policing objectives.
206 – Comply with health and safety legislation.
660 – Maintain standards for security of information.

Behaviours:

Respect for race and diversity
Team working
Community and customer focus
Effective communication
Problem-solving
Personal responsibility
Resilience

Introduction

Road traffic legislation can sometimes be complex. However, the legislation relating to driving documents is straightforward and easy to understand. Regardless of the type of vehicle a person is driving, he or she must hold a driving licence for that class of vehicle, and the vehicle must be covered by insurance and, in some cases, by a current MOT test certificate. The increase in the use of motor vehicles in our everyday lives has brought with it inherent problems for law enforcement agencies; the more vehicles being used, the more likelihood there is of road traffic-related offences being committed. These may range from what are termed minor traffic offences such as parking or document offences to more serious offences such as causing death by dangerous driving or driving whilst under the influence of alcohol or drugs. During this chapter we will look at how to use road traffic legislation in a practical way, focusing on how to deal with some of the minor traffic offences that you are most likely to encounter on a day-to-day basis.

As we work through this chapter it may assist you to have your own driving documents to hand, as we will examine each individually.

IDENTIFY THE PROBLEM

The scenario

It is 08:00 hours on a weekday morning and you have been directed to patrol outside the Castleton Infants' School, School Lane, following complaints from local residents about parking in the area between 08:30 and 09:00 hours.

RESEARCH THE PROBLEM

What do you know?

Local residents are complaining about parking in the School Lane area between 08:30 and 09:00 hours.

What do you need to know?

- ◆ Where are School Lane and Castleton Infants' School?
- ◆ Is there a contact to whom you can speak about the complaint?
- ◆ What are the details of the parking problem?

How are you going to find that out?

+ If you don't know, ask the communications operator over the radio.

+ Speak with the school.

+ Speak with local residents/complainants.

What next?

Acknowledge the call and make your way to School Lane and Castleton Infants' School.

At 08:30 hours you arrive in School Lane outside Castleton Infants' School. The school is located in a residential area and you notice that a vehicle has pulled up in front of the driveway of 32 School Lane, obstructing access.

On arrival you go into the school and speak with the head teacher. She informs you that this is an ongoing problem, and that she has complained to the police numerous times over the past two months. She states that people are parking/stopping wherever they please in order to drop off and pick up children from the school; this is causing traffic congestion outside the school that occurs at the beginning and end of the school day. The head teacher also informs you that the residents living opposite the school have complained to her about being unable to get in or out of their properties at the relevant times as people visiting the school are parking in an inconsiderate manner.

DEVELOP A PLAN

What do you know?

+ The vehicle has stopped in front of the driveway of 32 School Lane, obstructing the residents' access.

+ This is an ongoing problem that is affecting the school and local residents.

+ Road safety implications for children.

What do you need to know?

+ Is the vehicle on a 'road'? (A road is defined by s 192(1) of the Road Traffic Act 1988 as 'any highway and any other road to which the public has access, and includes bridges over which a road passes' (see **Appendix 2**). If School Lane falls within the scope of this definition, it is a road.)

- Apart from causing an unnecessary obstruction, are any other offences being committed or dangers being caused? (At this point there would appear to be no other offences committed. However, in similar circumstances it may be worth considering the offence of leaving a vehicle in a dangerous position as outlined in s 22 of the Road Traffic Act 1988.)

- Are there any other offences being committed (documents)?

- Who is the driver of the vehicle and who is the owner/registered keeper? (These are often different, particularly where the vehicle is a commercial vehicle, company car or even if the vehicle is just being used by a family member or friend.)

How are you going to find that out?

With regard to the last enquiry listed above, you need to identify the driver and speak to him or her in order to establish who drove and parked the vehicle. Remember, although establishing *ownership* of the vehicle will generally amount to preliminary fact-finding, trying to find out who parked the vehicle will amount to obtaining evidence about the person's possible involvement in an offence, and therefore requires the caution to be given if the answers are to be admissible later.

What next?

In respect of a person using a motor vehicle on a road, you have powers to demand and inspect certain driving documents. These include the driver's licence, certificate of insurance, and vehicle test certificate or MOT certificate. (For the definition of 'motor vehicle', see s 185(1) of the Road Traffic Act 1988.)

You approach the vehicle – a blue Ford Focus, index TB01 HRP – and see that it is unattended. After a couple of minutes, a man walks towards you from the direction of the school and unlocks the driver's door.

You are aware that this is a long-term problem and there are different approaches that can be taken to try to solve the problem. As there would appear to have been an offence committed at this time you decide to deal with this now.

❖ 112, 141, 101, 217

🗁 1A4, 2C1, 4C1, 1A2

Note: Behaviours, 🗁1A4, 4C1 and ❖141 should be covered in most circumstances as normal working practices.

IMPLEMENT THE PLAN

What do you know?

You know that the vehicle has been parked across a driveway and left unattended.

What do you need to know?

You need to identify the owner and driver of the vehicle, and establish if it is being used lawfully.

How are you going to find that out?

You need to speak to the man, explain why you are speaking to him, and ask him if he is the owner of the vehicle and if he parked it across the driveway.

What next?

At this point it is important to consider your personal safety when dealing with motorists. Try to avoid speaking to motorists whilst standing in the road. It is far safer to speak to the driver out of the vehicle, standing on the pavement or kerbside. If you are in a vehicle yourself, you could ask the person to sit in the back when you speak to him or her.

Remember that when dealing with any road traffic-related incidents/duties it is important for your own safety and that of other road users that you are clearly visible. It is advisable to wear reflective clothing; this may differ from force to force but is normally a jacket, bib, cap, strip, etc. Ensure that you do not get into a person's vehicle whilst they are in the driver's seat and in control of the vehicle. You may feel that you are 'only' dealing with a parking matter but this type of incident can often escalate into a confrontational situation. Always be aware of your personal safety and consider your conflict-management training.

You speak to the man at the side of the vehicle on the pavement. You explain that complaints have been received about parking when children are being dropped off at the school. When you ask for his details he gives his name as Kevin Mark O'Reilly; he states that he is the registered keeper of the vehicle and admits to having driven the vehicle and parked it across the driveway. You ask to see his driving documents.

He hands you a driving licence; you now need to examine it.

What do you know?

+ The man admits to having driven and parked the vehicle on the road.

+ He has handed to you a driving licence for you to examine.

What do you need to know?

+ Is the driver the named person on the licence?

+ What is his driver number?

+ Is the licence full or provisional?

+ What classes of vehicle is the holder authorised to drive?

+ Are there any conditions or restrictions on it (e.g. does he have poor eyesight)?

+ What is the date of issue of the licence?

+ What is the date of expiry of the licence?

How are you going to find that out?

By examining the licence thoroughly you will be able to find out the answers to the above questions. In addition, you should bear in mind that a driver may still have a copy of a driver's licence even though he has been disqualified from driving. You can find out whether a driver is disqualified by carrying out a Police National Computer (PNC) check.

Remember that you are carrying out an investigation into an offence. If you carry out a Police National Computer (PNC) check on the person it may also provide you with other useful information. This could include:

+ if they are previously recorded (known to police and what for);

+ if they are currently wanted;

+ any warning markers/signals that you may need to know about, e.g. violent, drug user;

+ last known address details, identifying features marks, scars, tattoos, etc. These may help if you are trying to ascertain if someone is providing the correct details to you.

In this case you carry out a person check and find that O'Reilly is not recorded, not wanted and not disqualified from driving.

So far as the licence itself is concerned, although the format has changed over recent years, all licences contain the same information. With the latest driving licence it is important to remember that it is necessary to check both the paper counterpart driving licence, D740, and the plastic photocard licence.

The first point to check is that the name on both parts is the same. On the paper counterpart this is shown on the first line of the address; on the photocard the surname (or family name) is at '1.' and the driver's first names appear at '2.'.

The driver number should be checked next. This is located on the paper counterpart in the top right-hand quarter and at '5.' on the photocard. The driver licence handed to you has the following driver number: OREIL 706132 KM9FS. The driver number is a unique number based on the person's name and date of birth. Here the driver's surname is O'Reilly, and the first five characters of the number – OREIL – relate to the first five letters of the surname. If the driver's surname comprises fewer than 5 letters – such as FOY – the two remaining spaces are filled with the number 9, so that this section of the number would then read 'FOY99'.

The middle section of the driver's number – 706132 – is formulated from the holder's date of birth. The first and last digits – the 7 and 2 – relate to the year of birth, so in this case the driver was born in 1972. The second and third digits – the 0 and 6 – refer to the month of birth, '06' referring to June. The fourth and fifth digits – the 1 and 3 – refer to the day of the month, i.e. 13th. You can now see that the driver's date of birth is 13 June 1972. This can be confirmed by checking the photocard at '3.', which shows the holder's date and place of birth.

If the driver is a woman, the number 5 is added to the second digit. Therefore, the second digit will either be a 5 or a 6 for a woman, or 0 or a 1 for a man.

The first two letters of the last five characters – KM9FS – refer to the driver's initials. The K and M here refer to Kevin Mark. If the holder has only a single initial, the figure 9 replaces a letter. The remaining three characters are for DVLA administrative purposes only.

The next matter to establish is whether the driver holds a full or provisional licence. This can be established by examining the photocard licence.

The categories of vehicles the holder is entitled to drive as a full licence holder are listed at '9.' on the front of the card licence. These are displayed again on the reverse of the photocard, along with the dates full entitlement was attained and the expiry date.

In this case the driver has a full licence for Category B, which entitles him to drive a motor car. As a full licence holder for a motor car, depending on the driver's age, this will also include authorisation to drive certain other categories of vehicle, including towing a trailer and driving certain goods-carrying vehicles.

Provisional entitlements are shown on the paper counterpart driving licence. If the licence is provisional for Category B motor cars, there are a number of conditions with which the holder must comply in order to drive the vehicle in accordance with the licence. These include:

(a) displaying 'L' plates on the front and rear of the vehicle, regardless of the class of vehicle. In Wales, provisional licence holders may display 'D' plates instead;

(b) being supervised by a person of at least 21 years of age, who has held a full licence for that class of vehicle for a minimum of three years.

The paper counterpart licence also contains details of the driver's history, including endorsements, penalty points, dates and types of offences.

On the photocard licence, the valid dates of the driving licence are shown at '4a.' and '4b.'.

If you are in any doubt whether the licence has been issued to the driver, there are a number of checks that can be made. These include checking:

+ the photograph on the card licence;

+ the driver number;

+ the name and address of the holder;

+ the date of birth of the holder;

+ the issue and expiry dates;

+ classes of vehicle the driver is authorised to drive;

+ the signature of the licence holder; and

+ the DVLA watermark on paper documents.

Having examined the driving licence, you now ask to see the driver's certificate of insurance. Mr O'Reilly hands a document to you.

What do you know?

The driver has told you that he is the owner of the Ford Focus, index TB01 HRP, and has also stated that he drove the car and parked it in School Lane,

Castleton. Under the terms used in the Road Traffic Acts, this could be phrased as 'driving a motor vehicle on a road'.

What do you need to know?

You know that in order to comply with the Road Traffic Act 1988, Kevin O'Reilly must have a valid certificate of insurance or cover note in respect of his use on a road of the Ford Focus, index TB01 HRP. Therefore, you are going to have to examine the document to check the following details:

◆ to whom it was issued;

◆ to which vehicle it relates;

◆ when it was issued;

◆ when it expires;

◆ what limitations as to use are imposed (if any);

◆ who issued it; and

◆ the policy number.

How are you going to find that out?

You now need to examine the document handed to you and check the details closely.

When you examine the document, you identify the following:

◆ the certificate was issued to Kevin Mark O'Reilly;

◆ it was issued in relation to vehicle registration mark TB01 HRP;

◆ it was issued at 00.00 on 24 September 200*;

◆ it expires at 00.00 on 24 September 200*;

◆ limitations as to use cover social domestic and pleasure, and use for the business of the policyholder;

◆ it was issued by Gladstone Insurance Services; and

◆ the policy number is MOT88245777528.

You are satisfied that the certificate of insurance is valid and covers the driver's use of the vehicle. You hand the document back to him.

As the vehicle has a registration plate which indicates that it was first registered more than three years ago, there is a requirement for the driver to have a valid MOT test certificate for that vehicle. If the vehicle has a personalised plate, or if you are in any doubt as to the date of first registration, you can always carry out a vehicle check using the PNC, which will give you this information and enable you to clarify the registered keeper's details as well.

You now ask the driver if he has a MOT test certificate, and he hands you another document.

What do you know?

You know the that the vehicle is Ford Focus, index TB01 HRP, and therefore it was first registered in 2001 and requires a valid MOT test certificate for its lawful use on a road.

What do you need to know?

The MOT test certificate contains information relating to the vehicle, including:

♦ the motor vehicle registration mark;

♦ the vehicle identification or chassis number;

♦ the Test Station number;

♦ issue date;

♦ expiry date;

♦ colour of vehicle;

♦ make of vehicle;

♦ approximate year the vehicle was first used;

♦ recorded mileage;

♦ if a goods vehicle, the maximum designed gross weight;

♦ type of fuel;

♦ tester's signature and printed name;

♦ certificate serial number; and

♦ authentication bar code. This has details of the Testing Station.

How are you going to find that out?

You now examine the certificate and note the following details:

♦ the motor vehicle registration mark is TB01 HRP;

♦ the vehicle identification or chassis number is HOL0000412V3107824;

♦ the Test Station number is 1BLE60;

♦ issue date, 5 August 200*;

♦ expiry date, 4 August 200*;

♦ the colour of vehicle as blue;

♦ the make of vehicle as Ford;

♦ the approximate year the vehicle was first used as 2001;

♦ the recorded mileage as 38454;

♦ if a goods vehicle, the maximum designed gross weight marked N/A;

♦ the type of fuel as petrol;

♦ tester's signature and printed name as 'P Morris';

♦ certificate serial number as JEO134840.

ACTION TO BE TAKEN

Now that you have examined all his driving documents, the driver apologises for parking across the driveway. You now need to decide what action to take. Your options are to report the driver for causing unnecessary obstruction, or to give words of advice. It is at this point that you will need to use your discretion to decide what action will be the most appropriate for the circumstances. You fully outline the issues raised by the school/residents and the possible safety implications for children and other road users. Kevin O'Reilly accepts this and apologises, stating that he did not realise the implications of his actions. Having taken all the factors into consideration, you decide to advise the driver regarding parking in the area in future and thank him for his co-operation.

What next?

You now need to make an entry in your pocket notebook in accordance with your own force guidelines. An example of this could be as follows:

08:30   *School Lane, Castleton. Patrol re parking complaints*

08:30   *Parked and unattended across driveway of 32 School Lane, Blue Ford Focus, index TBO1 HRP.*

08:33   *Kevin Mark O'REILLY, date of birth 13.06.72, 21 First Avenue, Castleton CL2 4PY. Driving licence number OREIL706132KM9FS. Returned to vehicle, admitted to being owner of Ford Focus index TBO1 HRP and parking across driveway. Driving Licence, Insurance and MOT certificates checked and in order. Advice given re parking.*

❖   112, 141, 101, 217, 127, 206

🗁   1A1, 1A4, 4G2, 2C1, 4C1, 2A1, 1A2

Note: Behaviours, 🗁1A4, 4C1 and ❖141 should be covered in most circumstances as normal working practices.

IDENTIFY THE PROBLEM

It is 08:40 and you resume patrol in School Lane. You see a vehicle pull up in front of another driveway. A woman and child get out of the vehicle and go into the school playground. You walk over to the vehicle, a red Vauxhall Astra, index V710 NWF, which has parked across the driveway of 7 School Lane.

RESEARCH THE PROBLEM

When the woman returns to the car, you ask her if she is the owner of the vehicle. She states that she is. You explain about the complaints regarding parking and tell her that she is causing an obstruction by parking across the driveway. You ask to see her driving documents; she replies that she doesn't have them with her, that she is in a hurry as she is running late, and that she doesn't want to be late for work.

DEVELOP A PLAN

What are your options?

Again the offence of unnecessary obstruction has been committed by the driver of the vehicle. Additionally, it is an offence for a driver to fail to produce his or her driving documents to a police officer on demand. Your options are to:

- issue a fixed penalty notice for causing an unnecessary obstruction;

- report the driver for both the offences;

- issue an HO/RT 1 form for the driver to produce her documents at a police station;

- give words of advice.

IMPLEMENT THE PLAN

As the woman is in a hurry and you gave words of advice to the previous driver, you decide to do the same here as regards the unnecessary obstruction. However, the driver does not have her driving documents with her.

You are able to perform a number of checks on PNC in relation to driving documentation. In this case you would like to check that the woman has a valid driving licence, insurance cover and MOT certificate for the vehicle (if required).

When a PNC vehicle check is conducted it will provide information details of:

- whether the vehicle is reported stolen;

- who the vehicle is currently registered to;

- any information markers on the vehicle, such as, used in commission of crime, stop and obtain details of owner/driver, registration plates stolen, etc.;

- a current MOT certification for the vehicle;

- whether a road fund licence is in place for the vehicle (road tax);

- insurance details can also be obtained; this check will tell you if a valid insurance policy is in place for the vehicle, any conditions of the insurance, details of the policy and insurance provider and who is named to drive the vehicle, etc.

When a PNC person check is conducted an officer can request a DL (driving licence) check. This check will provide details of whether or not a licence is held, what type of licence may exist and the classifications of vehicle that a person may drive on that licence, etc.

Tip: When conducting a DL check ensure that you have all details correct, such as spelling of names, etc., as the search criteria have limitations.

On most occasions these checks will be sufficient for you to decide how to progress a situation. However, if there are any discrepancies in the information or contentious issues such as medical grounds, vehicle classification, etc., then it is always advisable to examine the paper documentation. This would require the issue of a HO/RT 1 form in order for the original documents to be produced.

You request the aforementioned PNC checks from communications, they inform you that they are experiencing difficulties with PNC and cannot conduct the checks at present. You decide to issue a HO/RT 1 form.

What information are you going to require to complete the HO/RT 1 form?

The information you are going to require will include the following:

◆ name and address of the driver;

◆ the driver's date of birth;

◆ the vehicle's details, including make and registration;

◆ location of incident and, if different, where form HO/RT 1 was issued;

◆ the time and date of the incident;

◆ the time and date the request was made for the documents to be produced;

◆ what documents are required to be produced;

◆ the name of the police station at which the driver elects to produce the documents;

◆ your details as the officer requesting production.

ACTION TO BE TAKEN

By asking questions of the driver in relation to the above information you are able to record the following details:

◆ the driver's name and address is Rabinda Misra, 37 Castle View, Castleton CL2 8SY;

- the driver's date of birth is 14 March 1970;

- the vehicle is a red Vauxhall Astra, index V710 NWF;

- location of incident and issue of the form HO/RT 1 is School Lane, Castleton;

- the time and date of the incident and request is 08:40 am day/month/year;

- the documents required to be produced are driving licence, insurance certificate and MOT test certificate;

- the documents are to be produced at Castleton Police Station; and

- your details as the officer requesting production.

An example of an HO/RT 1 form is set out overleaf.

When making the request for documents to be produced, it is very important to make sure the driver understands what is expected. You may find it useful to use the following example of what to say:

> It is an offence to fail to produce your driving documents to a police officer on demand and you will be reported for that offence. However, if they are produced in order at a police station of your choice, within seven clear days, no further action will be taken.

The driver should then be cautioned as follows:

> You do not have to say anything. But it may harm your defence if you do not mention now something which you later rely on in court. Anything you do say may be given in evidence.

Remember to make a note of any reply the person makes.

Having completed the HO/RT 1 form, you must then hand the original to the driver to take to their chosen police station when they produce their driving documents. Most HO/RT 1 pads have at least two self-carbonating copies: the first needs to be forwarded to your administration department; the other one should be retained for your reference. Check at your station to establish where you need to send the administration copy.

After fully explaining the HO/RT 1 procedure you advise the woman regarding her manner of parking and the obstruction caused.

HO/RT 1 This form should be produced with your documents

Full Name (Driver/Supervisor/Other (specify) ....) Date of Birth

Ethnic Appearance ☐ (see cover for code descriptions)

Address

Postcode

Signature (Request only)

Location of incident	Time	Date

Location of requirement	Time	Date

VEHICLE

Registration Number.

Vehicle Description*

	Yes	No
Manual		
Motorway		
'L' plates		
Passengers		
Driver-supervised		
Rider with passenger		
Trailer		

If motorcycle, include cubic capacity; goods vehicle include gross and train weight if applicable; passenger vehicle include seats (not driver's)

Use of vehicle SDP ☐ Business ☐ Hire of reward ☐

Documents to be produced (see explanatory notes overleaf)

Check only   1 ☐ 2 ☐ 3 ☐ 4 ☐ 5 ☐ 6 ☐ 7 ☐ 8 ☐

Record details 1 ☐ 2 ☐ 3 ☐ 4 ☐ 5 ☐ 6 ☐ 7 ☐ 8 ☐

At:... Police Station

Issued by: Name: .... Rank and No.: ....Div. ☐ ☐

Reply to:

Central Ticket Office

Tick reason:

Accident	A
V.D.R.S.	V
Non. End. F.P.	F
Offence	O
Other	C

Having issued the HO/RT 1 to the driver, you now need to make an entry in your pocket notebook. An example of this might be as follows:

08:45	*Parked and unattended over driveway of 7 School Lane, red Vauxhall Astra, index V710 NWF.*
08:50	*Spoke to Rabinda MISRA, date of birth 14.03.70, 37 Castle View, Castleton CL2 8SY, who stated she was owner and driver of Vauxhall Astra index V710 NWF. Advice given re parking. Form HO/RT 1 (Exhibit PCS3112/1) issued for production of driving licence, insurance certificate and MOT certificate to Castleton Police Station. I said: 'It is an offence to fail to produce your driving documents to a police officer on demand and you will be reported for that offence. However, if they are produced in order at a police station of your choice, within seven clear days, no further action will be taken. You do not have to say anything. But it may harm your defence if you do not mention now something which you later rely on in court. Anything you do say may be given in evidence.' She made no reply.*
08:50	*Above pocket notebook entry completed in School Lane, Castleton.*

It is now 8:55am and the school day has begun; as a result the parking problems have ceased. You return to the school, liaise with the head teacher and update her regarding your actions this morning. She thanks you for your assistance and asks for your advice on developing a longer-term solution to the problem. You suggest that perhaps a meeting with the local neighbourhood policing team may be a way forward; she agrees and you state that you will refer the problem to the relevant team and a beat officer or PCSO will be touch in due course to progress the issue.

> ❖   112, 141, 101, 36, 42, 660, 217, 127, 206
>
> 🗁   1A1, 1A4, 4G2, 2C1, 2C3, 4C1, 2A1, 1A2
>
> **Note: Behaviours, 🗁1A4, 4C1 and ❖141 should be covered in most circumstances as normal working practices.**

IDENTIFY THE PROBLEM

It is now 09:15 hours and you resume patrol. You are walking into the High Street when you notice a green Peugeot 205, index S456 JAD, being driven in the direction of Church Lane. It pulls over outside J's Newsagents. The driver is sitting in the vehicle with the windows down and the radio playing loud music, which appears to be causing annoyance to some shoppers.

RESEARCH THE PROBLEM

What do you know?

The driver is sitting in the car, a green Peugeot 205, index S456 JAD, playing loud music which is apparently annoying shoppers.

What do you need to know?

◆ What offences, if any, are being committed?

◆ Is the driver both the owner and keeper of the vehicle, and does he have valid documentation?

◆ You also need to ascertain the driver's details.

How are you going to find that out?

You need to speak to the driver and ask relevant questions.

What next?

You approach the car and speak to the driver, the only occupant, through the passenger window. You ask him to step out onto the pavement. You state that the music is being played too loudly and appears to be upsetting passers-by. The driver turns the radio off. You ask him for his name and address, which he gives as Aaron Gavin Stringer, Flat 2, Peak Towers, Whatley Street, Castleton CL1 3KR. He gives you his date of birth as 20 April 1985.

You ask if he is the owner of the vehicle, and he says that he bought it two days ago for £200. He states that he has sent off the V5C Registration Certificate to DVLA and hands you the 'New Keeper Supplement' for the vehicle, with his details entered into the New Keeper's name and address section. You could conduct a PNC check to verify previous keeper details.

You then ask to see his driving licence, insurance certificate and MOT certificate. He hands you an MOT test certificate which you examine and, having checked all the key details, find to be in order. You then examine an insurance cover note issued to Aaron Stringer at 12 noon two days ago. It covers use of the Peugeot 205, index S456 JAD, for 30 days from the date of issue for social domestic and pleasure purposes. The issuing company is Wilson's Insurance and the cover note number is MOT543654.

The driver then hands you a paper and photocard driving licence relating to Aaron Stringer. Upon examination of the documents you note that the driver number is STRIN 804205 AG9DD. You also note that the driving licence is a provisional licence only for Category B cars. The car is not displaying 'L' plates and the driver was the only person in the vehicle.

DEVELOP/IMPLEMENT A PLAN

What do you know?

♦ You have seen a motor vehicle being driven on a road by Aaron Stringer who is a provisional licence holder for that class of vehicle.

♦ You also know that as a provisional licence holder, the driver must display 'L' plates to the front and rear of the vehicle, and be supervised by a person who is at least 21 years old and who has held a current full licence for that class of vehicle for at least three years.

♦ You know that there was no other person in the vehicle when you saw Aaron driving it.

What do you need to do now?

As you suspect an offence has been committed, you must caution the driver and make a note of the time before asking any further questions and pointing out the offences.

At 09:20 hours, you now say to Aaron Stringer:

> You do not have to say anything. But it may harm your defence if you do not mention when questioned something which you later rely on in court. Anything you do say may be given in evidence.

You may now point out the offences and say:

As a provisional licence holder you must display 'L' plates to the front and rear of the vehicle and be supervised by a person at least 21 years old who has held a current full licence for this class of vehicle for at least three years. You are committing an offence of driving otherwise than in accordance with a licence. In not complying with the terms of your licence you may also have invalidated your insurance cover.

To this he replies:

I'm sorry, I know. I've got my test in a couple of weeks and just wanted to get in some extra practice.

You must record this comment as a significant statement; remember he is under caution.

You can now report the driver for the offence by saying:

You will be reported for the offences of driving otherwise than in accordance with a licence, and no valid policy of insurance for this vehicle.

You should also caution the driver using the following version:

You do not have to say anything. But it may harm your defence if you do not mention *now* something which you later rely on in court. Anything you do say may be given in evidence.

The driver makes no reply. If a driver makes any reply, this must also be recorded.

ACTION TO BE TAKEN

What next?

It is also worth noting that the insurance cover for this vehicle may be invalidated because the driver does not hold a full licence and is not being supervised by a competent driver. If so, the driver commits another offence (of using the vehicle without a valid certificate of insurance).

In this situation you need to advise the driver that in driving now he will be continuing to commit the offence and that he should not drive the vehicle until he can comply with conditions as stipulated.

Aaron Stringer decides to lock the vehicle and return with his older brother later to collect it.

You now need to write up the incident in your pocket notebook. An example of this follows:

09:15   I was on foot patrol in High Street, Castleton when I saw a Green Peugeot motor vehicle, index S456 JAD, being driven towards Church Lane. The vehicle then parked on its nearside outside J's Newsagents. My attention was drawn to the vehicle as I could hear loud music coming from the vehicle, which appeared to be disturbing passers-by. I approached the vehicle and spoke to the driver, the only occupant, whom I now believe to be Aaron Gavin STRINGER, date of birth 20.04.85, of Flat 2, Peak Towers, Whatley Street, Castleton CL1 3KR. I informed him that the music was being played too loudly and was upsetting passers-by, at which he turned the radio off. I said 'Are you the owner of this car?', to which he replied stating he had bought the car two days ago for £200. I examined the 'New Keeper Supplement' with Stringer's details entered into the New Keeper's name and address section. I then said 'May I see your driving licence, insurance certificate and MOT certificate?' I then examined the MOT certificate, which I found to be in order. I also examined an insurance cover note issued by Wilson's Insurance, cover note no MOT543654, which appeared to be in order.

STRINGER then handed to me a paper and photocard driving licence in his name with driver number STRIN 804205 AG9DD. I also noted that the licence was a provisional licence only for Category B cars. The car was not displaying 'L' plates and Stringer was the only occupant.

At 09:20 hours, I said to STRINGER, 'You do not have to say anything. But it may harm your defence if you do not mention when questioned something which you later rely on in court. Anything you do say may be given in evidence. As a provisional licence holder you must display 'L' plates to the front and rear of the vehicle and be supervised by a person at least 21 years old who has held a current full licence for this class of vehicle for at least three years. You are committing an offence of driving otherwise than in accordance with a licence.'

STRINGER replied, 'I'm sorry, I know. I've got my test in a couple of weeks and just wanted to get in some extra practice.'

I said, 'You will be reported for the offence of driving otherwise than in accordance with a licence. You do not have to say anything. But it may harm your defence if you do not mention now something which you later rely on in court. Anything you do say may be given in evidence.'

STRINGER made no reply.

I advised STRINGER that in driving now he would be continuing to commit the offence and that he should not drive the vehicle until he can comply with conditions as stipulated.

STRINGER decided to lock the vehicle and return later to collect it with his older brother.

09:25   Return to Castleton Police Station.

Pocket notebook re above entry completed in Report Room.

In accordance with your local force policy you may at some stage be required to complete a Statement of Evidence based upon your pocket notebook entry. This will form part of the file for a summons to be processed. It would also be advisable to submit an intelligence report via the relevant force system.

❖   112, 141, 101, 36, 217, 127, 57, 206

🗁 1A1, 1A4, 4G2, 2C1, 2C3, 4C1, 2A1, 1A2, 2J1

Behaviours
Respect for race and diversity, team working, community and customer focus, effective communication, problem-solving, personal responsibility, resilience.

Note: Behaviours, 🗁1A4, 4C1 and ❖141 should be covered in most circumstances as normal working practices.

Assessment documentation

A **personal statement** prepared by you would be the most likely format for evidence from this type of scenario. If you had been in company with another officer then a **witness testimony** by them may have been used. The only witness in this case that you have to your actions is the head teacher who only actually witnessed part of your duties therefore could only comment on this small area. If an assessor had been with you at the time then they would have submitted an **observation report** outlining the NOS areas that they had awarded competence in.

In this instance you would produce a **personal statement** outlining exactly what you did and highlighting the units, performance criteria, knowledge and range that you wish to claim from this. The documentation you use will differ from force to force but there will normally be a specific form to be used. If you are unsure, seek advice from your assessor/supervision prior to submitting it for assessment.

The assessor will need to check that your evidence is acceptable and validate that it actually happened. As there are no witnesses to check with in this case, they will be looking at the **other evidence produced (supporting evidence)**, so you must also provide details of this on the personal statement. For this scenario this will be documentation such as:

Incident log ref. no.
Pocket notebook entry (include book and page numbers)
HO/RT 1 document re
PNC transaction numbers
Case/Process file number re STRINGER
Intelligence report ref. no.

If an assessor deems it appropriate they may ask **specific questions** regarding certain areas of the evidence for you to answer, these will be recorded, normally in written or voice-recorded format. This is generally done to clarify areas that may not have been fully covered or to look at specific criteria, range or knowledge that have not been achieved by performance. Another method that could be used to achieve this is **professional discussion**; this is similar, only it takes the form of a discussion between the candidate and assessor and is normally covering a greater variety of issues than questioning.

Power to require production of documents
Driving licence

Section 164 of the Road Traffic Act 1988 provides a constable with the power to demand production of a driving licence.

The following people may be required to produce their driving licences for examination, to enable a constable to ascertain the name and address of the licence holder, the date of issue of the licence and the issuing authority:

◆ a person driving a motor vehicle on a road (or the supervisor of a provisional licence holder);

◆ a person whom you have reasonable cause to believe to have been the driver of a motor vehicle at the time when an accident occurred owing to its presence on a road;

◆ a person whom you have reasonable cause to believe to have committed an offence in relation to the use of a motor vehicle on a road; or

- a person whom you have reasonable cause to believe was supervising the holder of a provisional licence when an accident occurred, or at a time when an offence was suspected of having been committed by the provisional licence holder in relation to the use of the vehicle on a road.

Certificate of insurance and test certificate

Section 165 of the Road Traffic Act 1988 provides a constable with the power to demand production of a relevant certificate of insurance and test certificate.

As a constable you may require the following people to produce their certificate of insurance and test certificate (if applicable) for examination:

- a person driving a motor vehicle on a road (other than an invalid carriage); or

- a person whom you have reasonable cause to believe to have been the driver of a motor vehicle at a time when an accident occurred owing to its presence on a road or other public place; or

- a person whom you have reasonable cause to believe to have committed an offence in relation to the use of a motor vehicle on a road (other than an invalid carriage).

That person must also give:

- his or her name and address; and

- the name and address of the owner of the vehicle.

Other offences

Section 87 of the Road Traffic Act 1988 defines the offence of driving otherwise than in accordance with a licence:

> (1) It is an offence for a person to drive on a road a motor vehicle of any class otherwise than in accordance with a licence authorising him to drive a motor vehicle of that class.

This offence applies when a person holds a particular licence and fails to comply with the conditions of the licence. For example, a holder of a provisional licence driving a motor vehicle when not displaying 'L' plates and/or when not being supervised by the holder of a full driving licence.

Regulation 103 of the Road Vehicles (Construction and Use) Regulations 1986 defines the offence of causing an unnecessary obstruction of the road:

No person in charge of a motor vehicle or trailer shall cause or permit the vehicle to stand on a road so as to cause any unnecessary obstruction of the road.

Flowchart – Driving documents

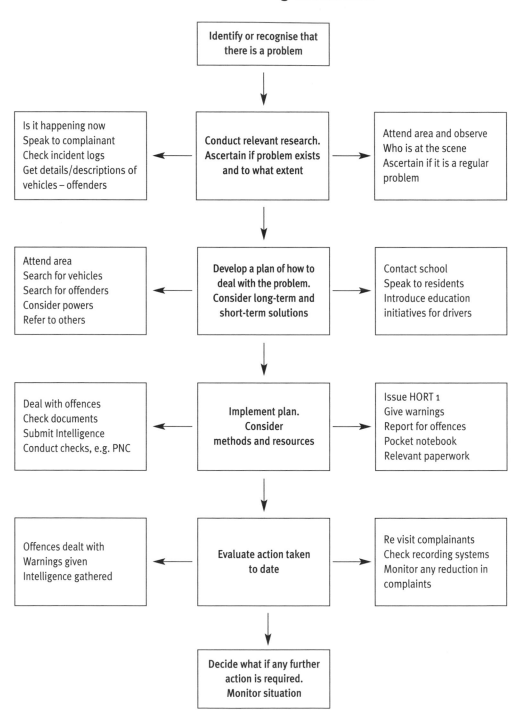

Identify or recognise that
there is a problem

Is it happening now
Speak to complainant
Check incident logs
Get details/descriptions of
vehicles – offenders

Conduct relevant research.
Ascertain if problem exists
and to what extent

Attend area and observe
Who is at the scene
Ascertain if it is a regular
problem

Attend area
Search for vehicles
Search for offenders
Consider powers
Refer to others

Develop a plan of how to
deal with the problem.
Consider long-term and
short-term solutions

Contact school
Speak to residents
Introduce education
initiatives for drivers

Deal with offences
Check documents
Submit Intelligence
Conduct checks, e.g. PNC

Implement plan.
Consider
methods and resources

Issue HORT 1
Give warnings
Report for offences
Pocket notebook
Relevant paperwork

Offences dealt with
Warnings given
Intelligence gathered

Evaluate action taken
to date

Re visit complainants
Check recording systems
Monitor any reduction in
complaints

Decide what if any further
action is required.
Monitor situation

Chapter 4
Youth Nuisance/Disorder

This chapter covers criteria within the following units of the National Occupational Standards for student police officers:

Level 3

1A1 – Use police actions in a fair and justified way.
1A4 – Foster people's equality, diversity and rights.
2C1 – Provide an initial police response to incidents.
2C3 – Arrest, detain or report individuals.
2C4 – Minimise and deal with aggressive and abusive behaviour.
2I1 – Search individuals.
2K2 – Present detained persons to custody.
4C1 – Develop one's own knowledge and practice.
4G2 – Ensure your own actions reduce the risks to health and safety.

Level 4

1A2 – Communicate effectively with members of communities.
1B9 – Provide initial support to individuals affected by offending or anti-social behaviour and assess their needs for further support.
2A1 – Gather and submit information that has the potential to support policing objectives.
2J1 – Prepare and submit case files.
2K1 – Escort detained persons.

It is likely that the following activities and behaviours from the student officer Role Profile will also be evidenced.

Activities:

112 – Conduct patrol.
141 – Promote equality, diversity and human rights in working practice.
101 – Provide an initial response to incidents.
36 – Conduct custody reception procedures (arresting officer).
35 – Conduct lawful arrest and process procedures.
42 – Prepare and submit case files.
74 – Provide care for victims and witnesses.
52 – Search person(s) or personal property.
660 – Maintain standards for security of information.
217 – Maintain standards of professional practice.
127 – Provide an effective response recognising the needs of all communities.
57 – Use information/intelligence to support policing objectives.
206 – Comply with health and safety legislation.

Behaviours:

Respect for race and diversity
Team working
Community and customer focus
Effective communication
Problem-solving
Personal responsibility
Resilience

Introduction

It is the Government's aim to create communities where residents feel able to go about their day-to-day business and to live their lives in safety. Sometimes these communities can be blighted by the activities of a minority. Invariably it is groups of youths gathering at certain points or in certain areas that cause fear among residents or people visiting the area. The disorder caused by these youths is referred to within the police service as youth disorder. Almost all forces view it either as a force priority or as a local priority to address, such is the impact it can have on communities.

IDENTIFY THE PROBLEM

The scenario

It is 20:30 hours on a Friday night. You are driving a marked police vehicle on mobile patrol with a colleague, PC Scott, when you receive a call from the communications centre requesting that you attend Wellfield Road, Castleshire, for a report of disorder by youths.

What do you know?

At 20:30 hours a call was received, alleging disorder by youths in Wellfield Road.

What do you need to know?

♦ What is the priority of the incident? This is relevant, because if it is a high priority call you have to respond within a specified time. The communications centre will need to know when you get there in order to log your time of arrival.

- Who was the call from?

- Do we have a name and address for the caller?

- Does the caller want to see the police?

- Do we have any more information as to the nature of the disorder or the number of persons involved?

- Do we have any descriptions of persons involved?

How are you going to find that out?

- Contact the communications centre for further information.

- If any names have been given by the caller, get the communications centre to use the computerised information system to check for any relevant details recorded against those names.

What next?

- Where is Wellfield Road?

- Are any other officers attending?

- Acknowledge the call and make your way to Wellfield Road.

The communications centre gives you further information, i.e. the name and address of the caller, a Mrs Grey of 20 Wellfield Road; she does not want the police to visit her home as she fears there may be reprisals against her for contacting the police.

The caller has further stated that the disorder is a regular occurrence; gangs of up to 20 youths regularly congregate outside the general dealer's shop.

You arrive in Wellfield Road and see a group of approximately 12 youths outside the general dealer's shop.

RESEARCH THE PROBLEM

What do you know?

You know you have a call about alleged disorder by youths.

What do you need to know?

♦ Is there any disorder, or are the youths just congregating in the street?

♦ Is it a genuine call?

How are you going to find that out?

♦ You cannot call at 20 Wellfield Road as the caller has asked the police not to attend.

♦ If you have not been seen, you could observe the behaviour of the youths.

♦ You could approach the youths and speak to them.

♦ You could go in to the general dealer's shop and speak to staff members.

What next?

♦ You decide to approach the youths and have a word with them. As you approach the youths you hear one of them swear and make noises like a pig; you are unable to ascertain which youth it was.

♦ You recognise two of the youths, having had dealings with them in the past for disorder and drunkenness.

What next?

On recognising two of the youths you radio the communications centre asking for Police National Computer (PNC) checks on any information or any warning signals for either of them. You remain out of hearing of the youths whilst waiting for the (PNC) check or use a radio earpiece, in case either of the youths is wanted on warrant or for any outstanding offences. You do not want them to be able to hear your radio when you receive the information from the communications centre. Your colleague, PC Scott, walks on to talk to the youths.

Remember, warning signals are entered on the PNC by officers who have had dealings with certain individuals in the past. They are a form of information system about an individual, and can flag up anything about an individual, from 'violent', 'assaults police' or 'carries weapons' to 'requires medication' or possibly 'self-harms'. They are a source of information for officers when dealing with individuals.

What next?

Be aware of the personal safety of both yourself and your colleague. There are 12 youths at the scene and you are aware that at least two of them have previous convictions.

At this point you may wish to update communications as to the current situation and your exact location. This will ensure that should you require assistance from other officers they will be sent directly to you.

Prior to commencing patrol you will have checked that you are in possession of all of your personal safety equipment and that it is in working order.

From your initial training be aware of and use the conflict management model, remember that this can used effectively to deal with any confrontation or conflict situation. Follow the suggested cycle of:

Information/intelligence received

↓

Threat assessment

↓

Powers/Policies

↓

Tactical options

↓

Actions

You also need to consider the impact factors for the offender/officer, such as size, sex, age, strength, skill level, alcohol/drugs, weapons, numbers, etc.

The check comes back from the communications centre. Both youths are recorded on the police systems: neither has any offences outstanding, nor are they wanted by the police for any offences outstanding, nor are they reported as missing from home.

On receiving the information you join your colleague by the youths.

❖   112, 101, 206, 660, 141

🗀   1A4, 2C1, 4G2, 4C1

Note: Behaviours, 🗀 1A4, 4C1 and ❖ 141 should be covered in most circumstances as normal working practices.

DEVELOP A PLAN

What do you know?

◆ You know that there is a group of about 12 youths outside the general dealer's shop.

◆ By their general demeanour they could have been causing disorder.

◆ The behaviour of one of the youths was disorderly as you approached.

What do you need to know?

◆ What have they been doing?

◆ How long have they been there?

◆ Who are they?

◆ Where are they from?

◆ Where are they going, if in fact they are going anywhere?

How are you going to find that out?

You talk to the youths but are not getting anywhere; they are not being noisy or insulting, but they are not being co-operative and are not answering questions, stating that they have not done anything wrong and are just standing about talking.

What next?

You have had a complaint that you need to investigate. Although the youths are being quiet at the moment, you need to satisfy yourself that all will remain quiet. You decide to go into the shop and ask the staff if everything is all right.

You speak to the shop owner and staff. The owner is an Asian man called Gurmit Singh; he has one member of staff, who is a white woman called Wendy James who lives locally. Both Gurmit and Wendy state that the youths have been outside the shop for the past hour and, although they have been a bit rowdy, they state that it is no more than the usual.

Both appear to be uneasy about talking to you.

They are either unable or unwilling to give you any further information.

You are not happy with this situation and believe that it is possible there is more to the situation than Gurmit and Wendy are prepared to tell you. At this point you decide not to pursue this any further as they are already reluctant to speak to you and you do not want to alienate them any further. Instead you tell them that you will deal with the youths outside and pay a return visit to speak to them further regarding the problem, at a more convenient time. You obtain full contact details and reassure them that you will help to deal with the ongoing problem.

You still need to sort out the situation as you have not yet resolved the complaint.

You are not happy with the youths staying outside the shop as you believe that they were causing disorder before you arrived and that they will continue to cause disorder after you leave. If you do not do something, the initial caller, Mrs Grey, will be dissatisfied with the police action.

You decide to have another word with the youths.

As you go outside the shop, one of the youths you know to be called Jaffa says something to his friends and they start looking at you and laughing. Jaffa is one of the youths you have had previous dealings with, and you have arrested him previously for being drunk and disorderly.

One of the youths throws a coke can in the air and kicks it across the road. The rest of the group laugh and look across at you and your colleague. You approach the youth and ask him to go and pick up the can; he replies, 'I am not a f***ing bin man; if it bothers you, you pick it up.'

You ask the youth his name; he replies, 'Donald Duck.'

IMPLEMENT THE PLAN

What next?

You again ask the youth to pick up the can; he refuses, stating that he pays your wages so if you are that bothered you can pick it up yourself.

You point out the offence of depositing litter and inform the youth that he should pick up the can and either keep it or deposit it in a bin, or you will issue a fixed penalty ticket for the offence and he will be liable to pay £50 approximately, or he can choose to be reported for summons. Dependent on the individual force the fixed penalty ticket for this offence may be administrated by the local council and the officer would be issuing the ticket on behalf of them. If this is the case, payment details will be outlined on the ticket issued.

(Reporting for summons is simply taking the person's details and the details of the offence for which you are reporting him, and submitting a file of evidence to put before the magistrates' court. The individual will be summonsed to attend court to answer the charges put to him by the court.)

Two of the other youths, one of them being Jaffa, start to swear, telling you to leave their mate alone. PC Scott warns Jaffa and his friend about their behaviour and informs them they will be arrested for a public order offence if they continue with their current course of action.

The situation appears to be getting out of hand.

What offences have been committed?

♦ The youth who has refused to pick up the litter has committed the offence of depositing litter in a public place contrary to the Environmental Protection Act 1990, s 87(1).

♦ Jaffa and his friend have committed an offence under the Public Order Act 1986, s 5(1).

ACTION TAKEN

What is your next course of action?

Think of your personal safety, your colleague's and others'. You contact the communications centre and ask it to send other officers to back you up.

The communications centre calls back immediately, stating that the task force van is nearby and is travelling to your location: estimated time of arrival (ETA) 3 minutes. You make sure that PC Scott is aware of the information and that he is safe. The task force consists of a number of officers (anywhere from 2 to 12) who are on call to assist with any incidents where more officers are needed, generally disorder calls. The title of this unit may vary from force to force. Some forces may not have these and assistance will be provided in a different manner.

You again speak to the youth who has deposited the litter, deciding to give him one last chance to pick it up; he again refuses and, egged on by his mates, is more abusive. In these circumstances you decide, as he is so unco-operative, he is unlikely to comply with a fixed penalty ticket. You caution him and inform him that you will be reporting him for summons for depositing litter. When cautioned he does not reply.

You ask him for his name and address; he replies, 'I have told you it's Donald Duck and I live in Disneyland.'

You inform the youth that if he does not give you his name and address you will arrest him for the offence of depositing litter and convey him to the nearest police station to ascertain his name and address for the service of a summons.

The youth now refuses to speak to you.

The Serious Organised Crime and Police Act 2005 introduced certain conditions that an officer must consider before arresting a person. This is referred to as the 'necessity test'. In order to arrest for the offence, the officer must be satisfied that one of the necessity test elements applies. The conditions are as follows, and may be remembered by using the mnemonic COP PLAN ID.

C arrest is necessary to protect a **C**hild or vulnerable person from another.

O arrest is necessary to prevent an **O**bstruction of the highway.

P arrest is necessary to **P**revent injury to that person or others.

P the offence is one of **P**ublic decency.

L arrest is necessary to prevent **L**oss of or damage to property.

A the person's **A**ddress is not known to the officer, or the officer doubts that the address provided is correct.

N the person's **N**ame is not known to the officer, or the officer doubts that the name provided is correct.

I arrest is necessary to **I**nvestigate the offence. The investigation must be conducted promptly and effectively.

D arrest is necessary to prevent the **D**isappearance of the person.

It is clear that the offence of depositing litter has been committed; you have reasonable grounds to suspect that the youth is guilty of the offence. The person's name or address is not known to the officer, or the officer doubts that the name and address provided are correct.

You arrest the youth for the offence of depositing litter.

What next?

You place the youth in the rear of the police vehicle, and you and PC Scott stand by it. Consider personal safety and what training you have been given for this type of situation. The youth Jaffa and his friend approach the police vehicle, shouting and swearing; you again warn them about their language and conduct, but they continue to swear at you and shout loudly. You inform them that you are arresting them under s 5 of the Public Order Act 1986 causing harassment, alarm or distress. They become even more aggressive towards you.

At that point officers on the task force arrive; you explain the situation to the officers on the task force van, and you caution and arrest the two youths, who are then placed in the task force van for transportation to the police station.

You return to your police vehicle to transport the youth arrested for depositing litter; you again ask the youth for his details, but he still refuses to speak to you.

The group of youths is still standing near to the entrance of the general dealer's shop. The youths are quiet, just talking amongst themselves. You ask them for their details and they are very compliant, giving you their names and addresses. You give them advice about their behaviour, inform them you will be back in the area in the near future, and then return to the police vehicle to transport the arrested youth to the police station.

Because of the youth's demeanour you believe that he may present a danger to you. Under s 32 of PACE 1984 and whilst not at a police station, you have a power to search the person who has been arrested if you have reasonable grounds for believing the arrested person may:

(a) present a danger to himself or others;

(b) have concealed on him anything which he might use to assist himself to escape from lawful custody;

(c) have concealed on him anything which might be evidence relating to an offence.

What next?

Using the approved search techniques you have been taught, you search the youth but do not find anything in relation to the areas outlined above.

You transport the youth to the police station.

What do you need to know?

♦ You need to be aware of the time you arrested the youth.

♦ The location of the arrest.

• The grounds for the arrest (necessity test and offence).

• The time of arrival at the police station.

The Custody Officer will need this information.

The Custody Officer will want to know if you have searched the person and may require a more detailed search to be carried out for safety reasons within the custody area.

You need to be able to give enough information to the Custody Officer for him/her to be able to make a decision about detaining the arrested person and what future action to take.

❖   112, 101, 35, 52, 206, 660, 141, 217

🗁 1A1, 1A4, 2C1, 2C3, 2C4, 2I1, 4C1, 4G2, 1B9, 2K1

Note: Behaviours, 🗁 1A4, 4C1 and ❖ 141 should be covered in most circumstances as normal working practices.

What next?

You outline the circumstances of the arrest to the Custody Officer, who asks the youth for his name, age and address.

The youth immediately gives his details to the Custody Officer. They are:

Paul Jones

28 Greenwood Gardens

Castleshire

dob 0302-- 16 years.

The Custody Officer instructs you to check the computer for the youth's details to verify his name and address, as the youth has no means of identification on him.

You check the computer and find the following information:

Police National Computer (PNC) Person by the name of Paul Jones dob 0302-- Resides at 28 Greenwood Gardens, Castleshire.

Jones is recorded as having previous convictions for theft, but he is not currently wanted or missing. He has no visible scars or tattoos.

Would that be enough to verify the person's details as correct?

You check the Force Computerised Information system and find that a 'Paul Jones 0302--' is again recorded on the system. Fortunately there is also a picture of Paul Jones on the system, and you can verify that the picture and the arrested youth are one and the same.

Some forces may now also have other technology available to help verify a person's detail, such as fingerprint scanning (Livescan). If available these should be used wherever possible.

What next?

You inform the Custody Officer of the verification of the details and the Custody Officer immediately tells you to report the youth for summons.

You remind Jones that he is under caution and inform him he will be reported for summons for depositing litter in a public place contrary to the Environmental Protection Act 1990, s 87(1). You could still issue a fixed penalty ticket as a method of disposal dependent on individual force policy.

Jones makes no reply when cautioned.

The Custody Officer completes the relevant paperwork (custody record) and Jones is released from police custody.

You will need to complete the paperwork for the litter offence, but prior to that you have to deal with the two youths you arrested under s 5 of the Public Order Act 1986. They have been transported to the police station by the officers who attended Wellfield Road to give you assistance.

You confer with the two officers who transported the youth Jaffa and his friend.

You confirm the time the two youths were arrested and the time they actually arrived at the police station. You also check to see if they were searched under s 32 of PACE 1984 and whether they have given their names to the transporting officers. You also need the names and numbers of the officers who transported the youths. All this information will need to be given to the Custody Officer.

What next?

You book the youths in with the Custody Officer individually, giving all the details you have and the circumstances leading to their arrest and the necessity test. Both youths give their full names, addresses and dates of birth to the Custody Officer.

The youth you know as Jaffa gives his details as:

Paul Orange

Date of birth 0406-- 15 years

Home address: 14 Albion Road, Castleshire

The second youth gives his details as:

David Webber

Date of birth 1907-- 16 years

Home address: 27 Albion Road, Castleshire

What next?

The Custody Officer tells you to verify the youths' addresses.

You check the PNC and find that both names are recorded: neither is wanted or missing; neither has any marks, scars or tattoos.

Both youths are recorded on the force computerised information system, but neither has a photograph on the system and the Livescan fingerprint scanning unit is not in use at this time.

Force policy may dictate that an officer does a physical check on the addresses given by arrested persons if they have no other means of identification on them. This is done to avoid arrested persons giving false details at the police station.

What next?

The Custody Officer authorises detention whilst the youths' details are verified. You contact the force communications centre and ask it to detail an officer to attend the youths' addresses to verify them. You are informed that due to the heavy workload it will be some time before a unit is available to attend to the detail.

You liaise with the Custody Officer who instructs you to attend the addresses and verify them yourself. You inform the communications centre that you will attend the addresses to verify the details of the arrested persons.

The Custody Officer also informs you that once the addresses are verified, you will need to arrange for an appropriate adult to attend custody in order for the youths to be dealt with. If there is no one at the addresses who is willing and able to attend then the Custody Officer will contact social services and arrange for them to fulfil this role.

You attend the given addresses of both the arrested youths and verify their details. You then return to the police station and report to the Custody Officer. An appropriate adult has attended for each of the youths concerned.

What next?

The Custody Officer is ready to finalise the two youths.

If the persons arrested had been adults (18 years or over) then it is most likely that, in these circumstances, they would have been dealt with by way of official/instant caution or charged with the offence and bailed to attend court on a specific date. In more complex cases a person would be bailed for advice to be sought from the Crown Prosecution Service (CPS).

In this case as the persons are juveniles (under 18), then depending on their previous history, it is most likely that they will be bailed to attend a reprimand clinic. This is where an official reprimand or a final warning will be administered. This will be recorded and will appear on the PNC. Juveniles can also be charged and bailed to attend court; however, this will normally be after advice has been sought from the CPS. It is generally used for more serious offences, prolific offenders or when a final warning has been issued previously.

In the presence of the relevant appropriate adults the Custody Officer bails the youths to attend reprimand clinic. You obtain fingerprints, photographs and DNA from the youths.

The Custody Officer endorses the relevant paperwork (the custody record) and reprimand clinic documents.

Both youths are then released from police custody.

You have paperwork to complete for the fixed penalty or summons for litter and for the arrests for s 5. You will also update the relevant information systems for your force, either on the computer or on paper. At this point you will also submit intelligence reports on the relevant system.

As previously discussed, you will have the paperwork to complete for the summons and the arrests, but what about the original call? Was it sorted out to your satisfaction, or – more importantly – was it sorted out to the satisfaction of the original caller?

What could you do?

When you have completed your paperwork, you could return to Wellfield Road and revisit the shop. You were not happy with the response of the owner and female staff member. Was there more disorder than they were willing to say? Were they intimidated at that time? If you called at the store at some other time, could you possibly get more information? There are possible offences which need to be investigated, for example offences contrary to the Protection from Harrassment Act 1997. Is there any indication of racially motivated offences?

What about the original caller – Mrs Grey of 20 Wellfield Road? Although she did not want the police to visit her at the time, she contacted the police by telephone, so the communications centre will have her number. Call her to see if you can make an appointment to visit her, or enquire whether she is willing to attend the police station to see you. During her original call she said that such disorder was a regular occurrence, so there may be a need for a greater police presence and possibly the need to gather information for other offences.

What about the local beat officer or community officers? They may have knowledge about the problem, or would certainly want to be made aware if there is a regular problem of disorder.

Although this evening you have made two arrests and summonsed a youth for an offence, have you sorted out the problem you were sent to deal with, or will it continue or even get worse for the persons concerned?

There are more enquiries and work to carry out before this job is finished.

What next?

You speak to the local beat officer who informs you that they are aware of the problem and there has not yet been a structured or planned approach to dealing with it in the long term. The only police action that has been taken to date has been short term such as the action you took by conducting arrests. The beat officer agrees to take on the problem and outlines that they will be taking a problem-orientated policing (POP) approach to try and provide solutions to the problems. It is likely that you have come across POP during your initial training.

Problem-orientated policing

Problem-orientated policing is a guide designed to help you gather information quickly, evaluate it and make best use of the information in order to identify responses to policing problems. POP focuses on specific crime and disorder problems with the intention of identifying the full problem and preventing the problem reoccurring in the future.

There are four main stages of POP, commonly known as SARA.

SARA and POP have been used for some time as a methodical process for problem solving. It is a widely used tool within community/neighbourhood policing arenas. There are four main stages.

Scanning is about spotting problems by using knowledge and basic data.

Analysis is using both initiative and information technology to dig deeper into problems, their characteristics and underlying causes.

Response is where a solution is devised, working with the community wherever possible.

Assessment is about looking back to see if the solution worked and what lessons can be learned from the process.

(Before embarking on a POP initiative always check to see if someone else has already tried to solve the problem. This could save you time and effort and help you to find out what worked and what did not.)

The beat officer explains that in relation to the problem with the youths they intend to implement the plan as follows:

Scanning Checking the incident log for number of calls, information from you regarding what the problem was when you attended.

Analysis Checking computer systems to obtain further details about the problem, incident logging of the nature of the problem, details of complainants, times and dates of occurrences. Any crimes/offences committed or dealt with. Obtain details of the youths involved and the actions or behaviour used that is causing the problem. By conducting high-visibility patrols and speaking to complainants/residents, shopkeeper/staff and the youths involved. Try and ascertain what the underlying causes of the problem are: is it boredom for the youths? Why do they congregate in that area?

Response This will be determined when the results from the analysis are received; it could entail increased patrols, liaison with youth workers, parish or local council to provide better facilities or environmental factors such as rubbish bins, increased lighting or seating, etc.

Assessment This will be performed after the response to identify areas that have been successful or not. Methods used could be monitoring amount of calls, police attendance, revisiting complainants, etc.

As has been highlighted, anti-social behaviour is not just a matter for the police to deal with by means of enforcement of the law. Although this is a powerful tool that can be used effectively in specific circumstances, as shown in the scenario, it will only provide a short-term solution. For a longer-term solution a more structured approach involving other agencies is required.

❖ 112, 141, 101, 36, 35, 42, 74, 52, 660, 217, 127, 57, 206

📁 1A1, 1A4, 4G2, 2C1, 2C3, 2C4, 2I1, 2K2, 4C1, 2A1, 1A2, 1B9, 2J1, 2K1

Behaviours
Respect for race and diversity, team working, community and customer focus, effective communication, problem-solving, personal responsibility, resilience.

Note: Behaviours, 📁1A4, 4C1 and ❖141 should be covered in most circumstances as normal working practices.

Assessment documentation

As you were in company with another officer then a **witness testimony** from that officer would be a good format for evidence from this type of scenario. (Remember that the officer will need to be competent themselves, preferably not a student officer, and you will not be able to Claim for any actions that PC Scott took.) Remember that the Custody Officer can also be used as a witness in relation to the custody based NOS. A **personal statement** prepared by you would also be an acceptable format for evidence from this type of scenario. If an assessor had been with you at the time then they would have submitted an **observation report** outlining the NOS areas that they had awarded competence in.

If in this instance you did produce a **personal statement** outline exactly what you did and highlight the units, performance criteria, knowledge and range that you wish to claim from this. The documentation you use will differ from force to force but there will normally be a specific form to be used. If you are unsure, seek advice from your assessor/supervision prior to submitting it for assessment.

The assessor will need to check that your evidence is acceptable and validate that it actually happened. They can check with a witness for a witness testimony or, if it is a personal statement, they will probably still check with the witness and also be looking at the **other evidence produced (supporting evidence)**, so you must also provide details of this on the personal statement. For this scenario this will be documentation such as:

Incident log ref. no.
Pocket notebook entry (include book and page numbers) by you and PC Scott
PNC transaction numbers
Custody record numbers
Case/process file number or fixed penalty ticket number
Reprimand files numbers
Intelligence report ref. no.
POP plans or referral forms completed

▶

If an assessor deems it appropriate they may ask **specific questions** regarding certain areas of the evidence for you to answer. These will be recorded, normally in written or voice-recorded format. This is generally done to clarify areas that may not have been fully covered or to look at specific criteria, range or knowledge that have not been achieved by performance. Another method that could be used to achieve this is **professional discussion**; this is similar, only takes the form of a discussion between the candidate and assessor and is normally covering a greater variety of issues than questioning.

Flowchart – Youth disorder

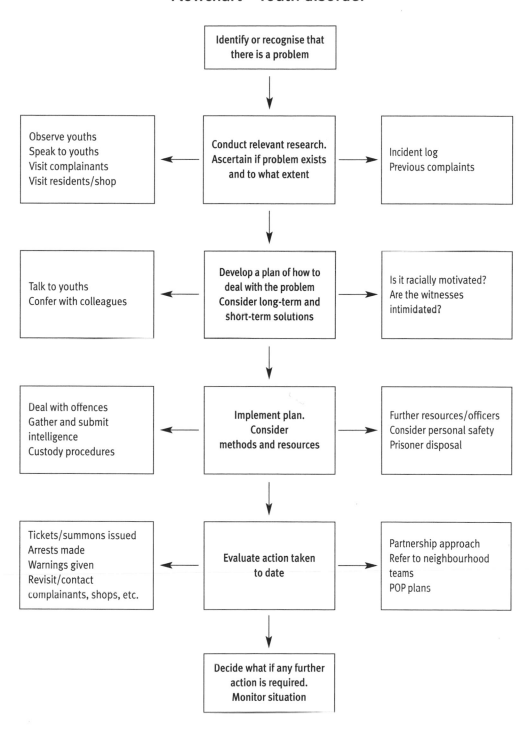

Identify or recognise that
there is a problem

Observe youths
Speak to youths
Visit complainants
Visit residents/shop

Conduct relevant research.
Ascertain if problem exists
and to what extent

Incident log
Previous complaints

Talk to youths
Confer with colleagues

Develop a plan of how to
deal with the problem
Consider long-term and
short-term solutions

Is it racially motivated?
Are the witnesses
intimidated?

Deal with offences
Gather and submit
intelligence
Custody procedures

Implement plan.
Consider
methods and resources

Further resources/officers
Consider personal safety
Prisoner disposal

Tickets/summons issued
Arrests made
Warnings given
Revisit/contact
complainants, shops, etc.

Evaluate action taken
to date

Partnership approach
Refer to neighbourhood
teams
POP plans

Decide what if any further
action is required.
Monitor situation

Chapter 5
Missing Persons

This chapter covers criteria within the following units of the National Occupational Standards for student police officers:

Level 3

1A1 – Use police actions in a fair and justified way.
1A4 – Foster people's equality, diversity and rights.
2C1 – Provide an initial response to incidents.
2H1 – Interview victims and witnesses.
4C1 – Develop one's own knowledge and practice.

Level 4

2G2 – Conduct investigations.
2I2 – Search vehicles, premises and land.
2A1 – Gather and submit information that has the potential to support policing objectives.
2G4 – Finalise investigations.
2J1 – Prepare and submit case files.

It is likely that the following activities and behaviours from the student officer Role Profile will also be evidenced.

Activities:

112 – Conduct patrol.
101 – Provide an initial response to incidents.
1 – Conduct investigation.
46 – Interview victims and witnesses.
74 – Provide care for victims and witnesses.
53 – Search vehicles, premises and land.
206 – Comply with health and safety legislation.
660 – Maintain standards for security of information.
217 – Maintain standards of professional practice.
141 – Promote equality, diversity and human rights in working practice.

Behaviours:

Respect for race and diversity
Team working
Community and customer focus
Effective communication
Problem-solving
Personal responsibility
Resilience

Introduction

Home Office figures estimate that there are around 210,000 incidents of people reported missing in the UK each year; the vast majority return safe and well within 72 hours, but thousands do not. These figures give an indication of the scale of the problem, which in turn highlights that a considerable amount of police time is allocated to dealing with these reports and the subsequent investigations that arise from them.

In 2006 the Association of Chief Police Officers (ACPO) from all 43 forces in England and Wales signed up to a national protocol agreement to be used when dealing with missing persons. This protocol covers the sharing and exchange of information between agencies that handle and respond to the issue of missing persons. It includes the creation and use of a comprehensive database of missing and unidentified persons in the UK. During major investigations the first hour is often referred to as the 'golden hour'; this is the key time to preserve evidence which if lost could impede an investigation. Research indicates that in child abduction cases that result in murder most children are killed within six hours of abduction. There is no time to lose and this must be borne in mind when conducting a missing person enquiry.

IDENTIFY THE PROBLEM

The scenario

You are on patrol; it is 16:00 hours on a Saturday when you receive a call to attend 3 Kingston Park, where Mr and Mrs May report their son Tim missing.

What do you know?

Are you clear about the information received? If not, now is the time to clarify.

What do you need to know?

To be able to provide an effective service you will need answers to many questions. It is your job to find those answers, but first be clear about what information you require.

Useful information would include the following (the list is not exhaustive).

♦ How old is Tim?

♦ Does he have any medical conditions?

- Where is he missing from?

- When and where was he last seen?

- Who was the last person to see him?

- Who was he with?

- Which locations does he frequent?

- Did he leave any message/note?

- Has he ever gone missing before? If so, where did he go and when did he turn up?

- Has his other, usual behaviour changed?

- Does he have a mobile telephone with him?

- Does he use the internet?

- What is he wearing?

- Description: what does he look like?

RESEARCH THE PROBLEM

How are you going to find that out?

Ask communications for any further information they may have. Then visit Mr and Mrs May, who have reported the incident to the police. They will be worried and you will need to bear this in mind when dealing with them. Nevertheless, you are conducting an investigation and need to obtain accurate information in an impartial manner.

You can do this by conducting an interview with Mr and/or Mrs May. Remember the initial interview sets the scene and parameters for the initial investigation and it may be necessary to interview others in addition to the person reporting. This may include friends, colleagues, etc., as these can often provide information not known to the person reporting.

It is important to conduct interviews efficiently and effectively, as this is the means of obtaining information that will be critical to the enquiry. The interview process should be continuous throughout the investigation, based upon information as it is received. All interviews need to be conducted sensitively, especially when dealing with emotional situations such as a missing person. In order to obtain the most information possible you need to use a form of questions called 'open questions'. This method is designed to elicit lengthy and full replies from the person being interviewed and is used when interviewing victims, witnesses or suspects. The opposite method, known as 'closed questions', will encourage limited or one-word answers.

For example:

Closed question – Is he wearing jeans?
Answer – Yes.

Open question – What type of clothing is he wearing?
Answer – Blue-coloured jeans, a red sweatshirt and a black jacket.

As you can see from the above example, the use of open questioning does in general generate more information from a person. Open questioning is sometimes referred to as '5WH'. The reason behind this being that the majority of open questions include the words:

Who – Where – Why – What – When – How

In the case of a missing person you are required to complete a specific form. This is normally titled a 'missing person investigation form', although the title may differ between forces, but the content will be very similar. The forms are based on the ACPO manual of guidance for the management of missing persons and the individual force policy for missing persons. The completion of this form will assist you with your initial interview and investigation and will ensure that you gather the information/evidence that you require in order to progress the investigation. The form also provides a base document to record all actions that have been taken and can provide continuity in a prolonged case between different police officers involved. You conduct an interview with Mr and Mrs May using open questions (5WH) whilst completing the form, and they provide you with the following information.

- A photograph of Tim that is a good likeness and has been taken recently.

- Full personal details of the missing person such as nicknames, nationality, date of birth, place of birth, height, telephone and mobile numbers and network provider.

- Full details of the initial informant (person reporting).

- Tim has not been reported missing in the past.

- A full description of Tim: white, male, he has no marks, scars or tattoos, short dark brown (natural colour) straight hair. He has no facial hair, medium build with blue eyes. Tim was wearing blue denim jeans, a red Adidas sweatshirt, black anorak-type jacket, white boxer shorts and black Adidas training shoes.

- Tim is wearing a gold stud earring in the left ear and a black wristwatch (make unknown); he will have a brown Adidas wallet containing his library card, school bus pass and money (about £5–10). He has no cash or credit cards and his passport is with his mother at home.

- As far as his parents know he or his friends do not have access to any vehicles.

- Tim is 11 years old.

Whilst children mature at different rates and each person must be treated as an individual, it is reasonable to assume that an 11-year-old child is vulnerable owing to his age and lack of life skills. You will also need to know whether he looks young or old for his age, as this may affect the way in which he appears to potential witnesses or offenders. He looks his age and is sensible.

- He is fit, healthy and not receiving any medical treatment.

It is very important to establish whether a missing person is suffering from any medical condition which, if untreated, would render him vulnerable and likely to come to harm. Consider a missing person with such a medical condition. What information do you require?

Useful information would include the following:

- What is the condition?

- What medication is required?

- What are the consequences if not treated?

- Does the missing person have medication with him? Check the quantity taken, as this can often indicate a person's intentions.

- He is missing from his home address.

- He was last seen at 11.00 am, he has been late home previously but has always telephoned first.

Times are important in placing the missing person. We now know that it is five hours since Tim was seen, fit and well, by his mother, and two hours after the pre-arranged meeting time.

- Is it unusual for Tim to be late?

- Would he normally make contact to explain any delay?

The time lapse can be critical if the missing person requires medical attention or medication. If that is the case then **you must inform your supervisor immediately**.

- Mrs May was the last person to see him.

- He was with his school friend, Martin Burke.

  What questions do you need to ask?

  - What is known about Martin Burke?

  - Home address?

  - Telephone number (including mobile)?

  - Places frequented?

  - Associates?

  - His address is provided. He frequents Bullocksteads Sports Centre. Mobile number. not known.

- Tim normally frequents Bullocksteads Sports and Youth Activity Centre to meet with friends.

- He told his mother that he would be back home at 2 pm as he was to go shopping with his friends.

- He did not leave any messages.

- His behaviour has not changed recently, he has never gone missing before and he appeared his normal self.

  Has anything in his life changed recently? It may be an incident/event regarded as insignificant by others but which has had an effect on Tim and which he chose not to discuss, or which he may not have had the opportunity to discuss with anyone.

  Is there anyone Tim confides in? Whilst you do not wish anyone to breach Tim's confidence, you must stress that Tim's welfare is the main concern.

  Mr and Mrs May state everything seemed fine, Tim would confide in them.

- He has a mobile telephone but there is no answer when it is called.

- He does not use the internet at home.

What next?

You have been given a lot of information and must assess each piece and its relevance to your enquiry.

> ❖ 112, 101, 46, 74, 141
>
> 🗁 1A4, 2C1, 2H1, 4C1
>
> **Note: Behaviours, 🗁1A4, 4C1 and ❖141 should be covered in most circumstances as normal working practices.**

What next?

At this point it is likely that you will become busy with the enquiries that need to be completed but the needs of those left behind should not be neglected. When a person goes missing this often creates considerable emotional stress on the remaining family or friends. Regular contact should be maintained in all missing person cases; this might involve the use of support agencies such as victim support, etc. In more serious cases a family liaison officer (FLO) may be provided.

You have been given a lot of information that you have recorded on the missing person investigation form; you now assess this information and decide how to progress the investigation.

DEVELOP A PLAN

An initial risk assessment must be made regarding the degree of harm the missing person is likely to experience. This will determine the urgency of the case and enable you and others to prioritise the tasks to be carried out. It must be recorded on the form and communications informed.

All missing person reports are potentially the first indication of a major crime. The vast majority concern missing people who return safely at some later stage; however, initially you must investigate if only to reassure everyone concerned that it is not something more serious.

The Association of Chief Police Officers' (ACPO) *Manual of Guidance* places risk in three categories:

◆ low risk;

◆ medium risk; and

◆ high risk.

Each of these categories is examined further below.

Low risk

Here there is no apparent threat of danger to either the subject (the person missing) or the public generally.

Once the person's details have been recorded on the Police National Computer (PNC) and the Police National Missing Persons Bureau has been informed, missing persons at this level of risk will not require any degree of proactive involvement by the police to trace them. However, the person reporting the missing person may still require support. In this respect, contact with the National Missing Persons helpline or other charities may prove of assistance.

Medium risk

Here the risk posed is likely to place the person in danger, or the missing person is considered to be a threat to himself/herself or others.

This level of risk requires some degree of proactivity by police and other agencies in relation to tracing the missing person and supporting the person making the report.

For example, if it was approaching the hours of darkness and Tim had no known places of refuge or means of support, money or food, and if he was wearing inadequate clothing, he would be likely to suffer as a result.

High risk

In these cases:

(a) the risk posed is immediate and there are substantial grounds for believing that the person is in danger through his or her own vulnerability or mental state; *or*

(b) the risk posed is immediate and there are substantial grounds for believing that the public is in danger due to the person's mental state.

A high-risk situation will require the immediate deployment of police resources and a member of your senior management team to be involved in press/media strategy and/or close contact with outside agencies.

For example, if Tim required life-saving medication and it was known that he did not have it with him, this would constitute a high-risk situation. Timings are critical and it is likely that you would be guided by your supervisor and senior management.

Making the initial risk assessment

The information that you obtain is critical in forming an accurate risk assessment for this report, and in ensuring that the investigation receives the correct level of attention.

Based on the information that you now have, complete an initial risk assessment, making notes to substantiate your decision.

When considering risk assessment, take into account the following:

Is there anything to suggest that the missing person is likely to cause self-harm or attempt suicide?

+ Has he or she done this before?

+ Does he or she have the means to carry out such harm?

+ Has any communication the missing person has left (or the absence of it) given cause for concern?

+ Was the person's mental and/or physical state vulnerable or unstable when he or she was last seen?

If the answers to any of these questions are 'Yes', then consider the following:

+ Where does the person like to go (favourite places)?

+ Is there anywhere of emotional significance for him or her, e.g. family grave?

+ Are there any places in the locality favoured by people committing suicide, e.g. cliffs, bridges, railways?

Is the person believed to have been the victim of a crime?

This is very difficult to judge with any certainty. If you think that the person might have been a victim, consider conducting house-to-house enquiries for any information that would assist in your assessment. Remember the 'Golden Hour' and contact your supervisor immediately. The need for specialist search teams will be considered by your supervisor based upon the information that you have obtained.

Is the person vulnerable by reason of age or infirmity?

Many young people appear to be 'streetwise', but it is important to remember that legally they are children and that they do not have the same abilities to look after themselves as do adults. Elderly people often become confused and may not be able to cope when removed from their normal environment.

Is the person suffering from some physical disability or mental illness?

Many people suffering from mental illness may have a distorted view of reality that can result in irrational behaviour. Consider seeking professional medical guidance.

Has the person been subject to bullying?

Bullying is the cause of an increasing number of suicides, especially amongst children.

Based on the information you have been given, it is likely that Tim is considered to be 'medium risk', for the following reasons:

- He is 11 years old.

- He would not normally be late for pre-arranged appointments.

- He has not been missing previously.

- He is not responding to attempts to contact him via mobile phone.

- This is out of character for Tim.

Whilst at this stage the 'medium risk' categorisation may be appropriate, it is important to remember that risk assessment is an ongoing, dynamic activity. It must be continually reviewed as and when any new information comes to your attention.

IMPLEMENT THE PLAN

What do you know?

- That Tim is definitely a missing person; he has gone missing from his home address.

- You have conducted an interview with his parents, used 5WH, and completed as much of the missing person investigation form as possible at this stage. As a result of this you have gathered personal information about Tim including a detailed description, details of friends and places that he frequents.

- That Tim has a mobile phone with him but there is no answer when you ring it.

What do you need to know?

- If there is any further evidence at the home address that you may need to assist with the investigation.

- Do Tim's friends have any idea where he may be?

- Has Tim been to any of the places that he normally frequents?

- Can Tim be traced via his mobile phone?

- You have completed a risk assessment and Tim is at present 'medium risk'.

How are you going to find that out?

- *Perform a search of the home address*. One of the most important points to consider when investigating a report of a missing person is 'to clear the ground from under your feet', a very basic but crucial course of action. It is not unusual for people to be reported missing when in fact they are still in the premises. Young children in particular have been found in cupboards, under beds, even in lofts.

  Be methodical with your searching, even if the person reporting assures you that they have checked everywhere. Sensitively explain that you need to check all of the property. Thoroughly search all rooms, large cupboards, under stair-wells, beds, lofts, etc. Check gardens, outbuildings and anywhere that could conceal a person.

  As well as providing a physical check, conducting a thorough search affords you the opportunity to build a picture of the missing person's lifestyle, habits and interests. This gives you the opportunity to discuss with the person reporting any issues that may provide information that has not been obtained from the initial interview.

  House-to-house enquiries. By performing house-to-house enquiries in the surrounding area you may gain further information regarding the missing person and eliminate any locations that they may be at, such as a neighbour's house, at the corner shop, in the park, etc.

- Visit the friends that have been discussed and perform initial interviews with them or any family/friends that may be present in their absence.

- Perform checks on the places outlined that the missing person normally frequents, speak to persons at the places and gather any relevant information.

- In relation to the mobile phone you could consider asking your supervisor to contact the mobile service provider. All forces have a nominated person, a single point of contact (SPOC) responsible for liaison. By registering the number of the missing person's phone, if the phone is used at any time then a time, date and location can be identified. This information would greatly assist in any search for Tim; however, this is a serious step in the investigation. To instigate this action involves interference with a person's right to respect for a private and family life, home and correspondence under article 8 of the Human Rights Act 1998. However, should the risk to the missing person be serious then any action would be justified, necessary and proportionate; in addition, article 2 of the same Act (right to life) would afford protection.

What next?

You perform a thorough search of the home address and do not find any further information or evidence.

House-to-house enquiries in the road where Tim resides, Kingston Park, reveal that a neighbour saw Tim at the bus stop around the corner at 11:30 am. He was with another male about the same age as him, who from the description would seem to be Martin Burke. They told her that they were waiting to catch a bus. Tim seemed in good spirits: at that point the boys were laughing and joking.

You arrange for a colleague to attend the home address of Martin Burke and conduct an initial interview with his parent/guardian or Martin if he is present.

You attend the Bullocksteads Sports Centre to obtain any further information regarding Tim.

Your supervisor outlines that at this point in the investigation Tim is risk-assessed as medium risk; therefore they are unable to authorise a SPOC enquiry regarding use of his mobile phone at this point.

ACTION TAKEN

What do you know?

+ House search has been performed and was negative.

+ House-to-house highlighted that Tim and another boy, possibly Martin Burke, were seen fit and well at the bus stop close to Tim's home address at 11:30 am.

+ SPOC mobile phone enquiry is not authorised at present.

+ Enquiries have been initiated regarding Martin Burke and the sports centre.

+ You have updated supervision regarding the progress of the investigation and have endorsed the missing person investigation form with all actions taken.

What do you need to know?

◆ The results of any enquiries that have been completed.

How are you going to find that out?

◆ Contact the officers carrying out the enquiries for an update.

What next?

Your colleague who attended Martin Burke's address informs you that they have spoken to his mother, who stated that he said he was going shopping earlier with his friend Tim May. He then said that if he had enough money left they would go for a game of snooker at the sports centre. She is not unduly worried about Martin, as he was not due back in the house until 20:00 hrs; he does not have a mobile phone.

Whilst at the Bullocksteads Sports Centre you liaise with the staff and inform them of the situation. The manager informs you that they do have CCTV on the entrance to the sports centre and it can be viewed for that day if required.

The staff are shown the photograph you have of Tim and they assist you in a search of the premises: you find Tim fit and well playing snooker in the recreation area. You contact his parents by telephone and inform them that you will give him a lift home. You take both Martin and Tim to their respective home addresses.

❖   112, 101, 1, 46, 74, 141, 206, 53, 217

🗁 1A1, 1A4, 2C1, 2H1, 4C1, 2G2, 212

Note: Behaviours, 🗁1A4, 4C1 and ❖141 should be covered in most circumstances as normal working practices.

You need to conduct a return interview with Tim.

When a missing person returns, the person reporting the incident often experiences many emotions, including anger. You must assess the situation and be sensitive to this fact, as your handling of this situation can have a major bearing on the quality of your interview.

Remember, people go missing for a variety of reasons, sometimes as a result of abuse by a family member or carer. If the interview is conducted in the presence of the abuser, the missing person is unlikely to discuss the real reasons for his or her disappearance. In such cases you will need the assistance of an 'appropriate adult', e.g. an approved social worker. Further, it could compound matters by returning the person to the place of abuse. If you suspect abuse of a vulnerable person, seek the assistance of specially trained officers from your force's vulnerability unit to ensure that the best interests of the vulnerable person are safeguarded.

In this particular case you have no reason for concern. Mr and Mrs May are relieved that Tim has been returned fit and well and are very grateful to you for your time and efforts. During the return interview Tim admits that he has had his mobile phone switched to silent ring by mistake and did not hear any of the calls made by his parents. He went shopping as planned and then decided to play snooker with his friends at the sports centre; he became involved in an informal tournament and totally lost track of the time. You are happy with this explanation, record the details onto the missing person investigation form and finalise the investigation. You update communications and supervision and submit the form through the designated channel. The information on the form is not only important for a current investigation: others will rely upon it if Tim goes missing again. Any intelligence reports should be submitted via the relevant system.

Each time you deal with a missing person report or enquiry it should be treated as an investigation (it is not just a form-filling exercise). All the investigative tools that you have at your disposal should be used as in any other type of investigation. In this case these included interviewing, house-to-house, searching, SPOC enquiries, CCTV, friends, family, descriptions, etc.

Most missing person reports that you attend will follow a similar format and come to a satisfactory conclusion as in this scenario; however, some will not. It is for these situations that the process you have just followed will become invaluable as they may progress into major investigations or highlight abuse, abduction or even murder; the initial action taken in the 'golden hour' is fundamental to this process.

❖ 112, 101, 1, 46, 74, 53, 206, 660, 217, 141

📁 1A1, 1A4, 2C1, 2H1, 4C1, 2A1, 2G2, 2I2, 2G4, 2J1

Behaviours
Respect for race and diversity, team working, community and customer focus, effective communication, problem-solving, personal responsibility, resilience.

Note: Behaviours, 📁1A4, 4C1 and ❖141 should be covered in most circumstances as normal working practices.

Assessment documentation

A **personal statement** prepared by you would be the most likely format for evidence from this type of scenario. If you had been in company with another officer then a **witness testimony** by them might have been used. The only witness in this case that you have to your actions is the supervisor who could comment on the updates and requests made and the completion of the form. In this type of scenario, as all actions taken by you are recorded on the missing person form, this could also be submitted as **product evidence** to claim some areas. If an assessor had been with you at the time then they would have submitted an **observation report** outlining the NOS areas that they had awarded competence in.

In this instance you would produce a **personal statement** outlining exactly what you did and the missing person form as **product evidence** highlighting the units, performance criteria, knowledge and range that you wish to claim from these. The documentation you use will differ from force to force but there will normally be a specific form to be used. If you are unsure, seek advice from your assessor/supervisor prior to submitting it for assessment.

The assessor will need to check that your evidence is acceptable and validate that it actually happened. They can check with a witness regarding what they can verify and will also look at the **other evidence produced (supporting evidence)**, so you must also provide details of this on the personal statement. For this scenario this will be documentation such as;

Incident log ref. no.
Pocket notebook entry (include book and page numbers) for you and other officers
Missing person investigation form ref. no. (if copy not already produced)
Intelligence report ref. no.
Search forms or documents completed ref. no.
Any documents completed in relation to viewing CCTV evidence.

If an assessor deems it appropriate they may ask **specific questions** regarding certain areas of the evidence for you to answer; these will be recorded, normally in written or voice-recorded format. This is generally done to clarify areas that may not have been fully covered or to look at specific criteria, range or knowledge that have not been achieved by performance. Another method that could be used to achieve this is **professional discussion**; this is similar, only it takes the form of a discussion between the candidate and assessor and is normally covering a greater variety of issues than questioning.

Flowchart – Missing persons

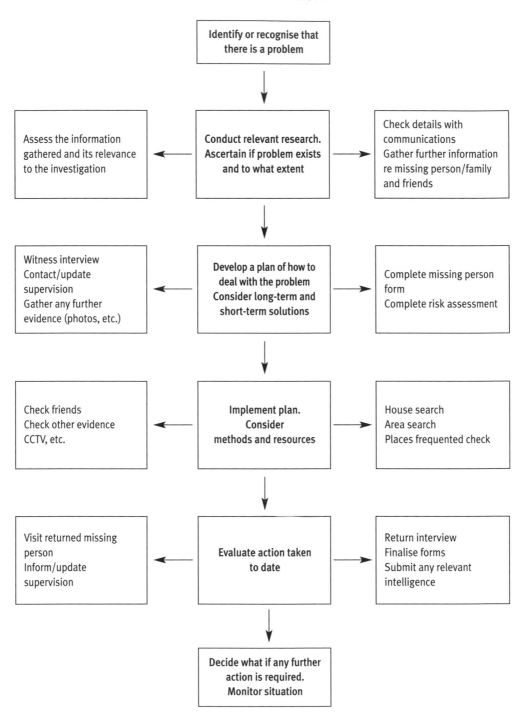

	Identify or recognise that there is a problem	
Assess the information gathered and its relevance to the investigation	Conduct relevant research. Ascertain if problem exists and to what extent	Check details with communications. Gather further information re missing person/family and friends
Witness interview. Contact/update supervision. Gather any further evidence (photos, etc.)	Develop a plan of how to deal with the problem. Consider long-term and short-term solutions	Complete missing person form. Complete risk assessment
Check friends. Check other evidence CCTV, etc.	Implement plan. Consider methods and resources	House search. Area search. Places frequented check
Visit returned missing person. Inform/update supervision	Evaluate action taken to date	Return interview. Finalise forms. Submit any relevant intelligence
	Decide what if any further action is required. Monitor situation	

Chapter 6
Shoplifting

This chapter covers criteria within the following units of the National Occupational Standards for student police officers:

Level 3

1A1 – Use police actions in a fair and justified way.
1A4 – Foster people's equality, diversity and rights.
2C1 – Provide an initial police response to incidents.
2C3 – Arrest, detain or report individuals.
2H1 – Interview victims and witnesses.
2I1 – Search individuals.
2K2 – Present detained persons to custody.
4C1 – Develop one's own knowledge and practice.
4G2 – Ensure your own actions reduce the risks to health and safety.

Level 4

2A1 – Gather and submit information that has the potential to support policing objectives.
2G2 – Conduct investigations.
2G4 – Finalise investigations.
2H2 – Interview suspects.
2I2 – Search vehicles, premises and land.
2J1 – Prepare and submit case files.
2K1 – Escort detained persons.

It is likely that the following activities and behaviours from the student officer Role Profile will also be evidenced.

Activities:

112 – Conduct patrol.
41 – Complete prosecution procedures.
141 – Promote equality, diversity and human rights in working practice.
101 – Provide an initial response to incidents.
36 – Conduct custody reception procedures (arresting officer).
35 – Conduct lawful arrest and process procedures.
42 – Prepare and submit case files.
1 – Conduct investigation.
45 – Interview suspects.
46 – Interview victims and witnesses.
52 – Search person(s) or personal property.

53 – Search vehicles, premises and land.
660 – Maintain standards for security of information.
217 – Maintain standards of professional practice.
127 – Provide an effective response recognising the needs of all communities.
57 – Use information/intelligence to support policing objectives.
206 – Comply with health and safety legislation.

Behaviours:

Respect for race and diversity
Team working
Community and customer focus
Effective communication
Problem-solving
Personal responsibility
Resilience

Introduction

The offence of 'shoplifting' does not actually exist in legislation or statute. It is a term applied to a form of theft whereby a person steals property from a shop or store. The offence crosses social boundaries and costs the retail industry millions of pounds a year. It can be commited by all sorts of people, ranging from well-organised gangs who steal to order from others, to those from affluent backgrounds, to schoolchildren or elderly people. The offence cannot be assigned to one particular group.

As a student police officer, it is highly likely that you will be called to deal with shoplifters on a regular basis.

IDENTIFY THE PROBLEM

The scenario

It is 14:30 hours on a weekday afternoon and you are on patrol. You receive a call from the communications centre directing you to attend Nixon's department store. The security staff have detained an adult male shoplifter and are requesting police attendance.

What do you know?

At 14:30 hours today a call was received requesting police attendance at Nixon's department store, where a male shoplifter has been detained by security staff.

What do you need to know?

- Where is Nixon's department store?
- Where has the shoplifter been detained within the store?

How are you going to find that out?

If you do not already know, ask the communications operator over the radio.

What next?

Acknowledge the call and make your way to the security office at the department store.

At 14:35 hours you arrive outside the security office at Nixon's department store. You inform the communications centre that you have arrived. You enter the security office where you see Maria Whatley, the store detective, in company with the suspect. You say to the suspect, 'Listen to what the store detective has to say.' The store detective then says, in the presence and hearing of the suspect: 'I saw this man in the men's wear department, where he removed a leather jacket from its hanger, put it on and then left the store, making no attempt to pay. Outside the store, I challenged him and asked him to accompany me back to the security office.' The leather jacket has a 'Nixon's' barcode label attached to it and is priced at £149.99.

RESEARCH THE PROBLEM

What do you know?

The suspect was seen by the store detective to select a jacket from a display, put it on and then leave the store, making no attempt to pay for the jacket.

What do you need to know?

- Has an offence been committed?
- If so, what offence?
- What do I need to know and what are my powers?

How are you going to find that out?

The store detective alleges that the suspect has stolen the jacket, which is theft. You have already been told what the store detective has seen.

At this stage you need to be satisfied that you have reasonable suspicion that the offence of theft has been committed. As the store detective has informed you that she saw the suspect take the jacket from a display and leave the store making no attempt to pay, this would amount to reasonable suspicion that a theft has occurred.

What next?

The man gives his name as Jake Rowlands, aged 25, and an address at Flat 3, Kirsten Court, Castleton; he has no identification on him. The store contacted the police and wants to prosecute.

Is it necessary to use your power of arrest? What factors do you need to consider?

(Remember the necessity test 'COP PLAN ID' in Chapter 4.)

DEVELOP A PLAN

What do you know?

♦ You have a name and address for the suspect.

♦ The store wishes the police to take action and prosecute.

What do you need to know?

♦ You need to confirm the suspect's details.

♦ You can arrest the suspect only if it fits the conditions of the necessity test. You should therefore consider what alternatives you have.

Your options are:

(a) Return the property and use your discretion to release the suspect with a verbal warning;

(b) to report him for further action to be taken by way of summons; or

(c) to arrest for the offence of theft.

How are you going to find that out?

◆ You can confirm the suspect's details by using the various computer systems available. For example, the Police National Computer (PNC), voters' register or other computer system used by your own force. Do they have any ID documents on them such as driving licence, passport, etc.?

◆ In deciding how to deal with the suspect, you should take into account the seriousness of the offence and the wishes of the victim (the store). Also what you will need to do in order to complete the investigation.

What next?

Having taken account of all the above factors, you make the decision to arrest the suspect, as in accordance with the necessity test arrest is necessary to investigate the offence.

It is very important that the suspect clearly understands what you are doing and that he is informed of the caution. It is also important to note the suspect's reaction to what the store detective tells you in the presence and hearing of the suspect.

An example of what you might say is:

> You have heard what the store detective has had to say. I am arresting you on suspicion of theft of the jacket. You do not have to say anything. But it may harm your defence if you do not mention when questioned something which you later rely on in Court. Anything you do say may be given in evidence.

The suspect makes no reply.

You also need to record the time and place that this occurred.

Should the suspect have made a reply when cautioned, you will need to record this, on a piece of paper (that will later be placed in property), in your pocket notebook or on the custody record when you are booking the suspect into custody.

If at any time whilst you are dealing with a suspect and they make a comment about the offence that you feel may be relevant to the case, you should treat this as a significant statement. A significant statement should be recorded as outlined previously and once it has been recorded the suspect should be given the opportunity to read this and sign it as a correct account. The fact that a significant statement has been made and what was said should be outlined to the custody officer when they are accepting custody of the suspect. It should also be revisited during any subsequent interview in order for it to be used as evidence in the case.

IMPLEMENT THE PLAN

What do you know?

You have now arrested the suspect on suspicion of theft of the jacket.

What do you need to know?

♦ Transport to the police station needs to be requested, along with an estimate of how long it will take to arrive.

♦ Does the suspect have any other stolen property, or items which could pose a potential danger to you or himself?

♦ What is the proper procedure in relation to the seizure of the stolen property, i.e. the jacket?

♦ Is this person wanted, do they have any violence markers, etc.,…are they even recorded on PNC?

How are you going to find that out?

♦ Using your personal radio, contact the communications centre to request transport and an estimated time of arrival (ETA). Conduct a PNC person check.

♦ The suspect is now in your care and custody. Under s 32 of PACE 1984 (see **Appendix 2**), whilst not at a police station you have a power to search the person who has been arrested for specific reasons, as outlined in Chapter 4.

♦ The jacket is evidence that an offence has been committed and is an exhibit. All exhibits need to be clearly labelled and given an identification number which relates to the person who is to produce the item as an exhibit. This person is the first witness who has had contact with the item. In this example, the store detective has taken possession of the item in the security office and will be the person to produce the item at a court hearing. The item is given the exhibit number, which will include the store detective's initials and a consecutive number. Some forces do this differently from others.

In this case the exhibit reference will be MEW/1; this represents the store detective's initials (Maria Elizabeth Whatley) and the number 1, indicating that it is the first item she dealt with in this case. A label will then be completed using this reference, which will be signed by each person who has had possession of the property. It is necessary for the item to be retained and kept available for any subsequent court hearing. If the items in question are perishable (e.g. food products), they can be photographed and the photo produced as an exhibit. With items such as clothing, you may be able to seize the item, retain it and book it into the property store at your station, or the store detective may sign a property retention form, promising to retain the item until the conclusion of any court proceedings.

What next?

You have requested transport and been told that a unit will be with you in 10 minutes. You conduct a search of the person and you are satisfied that the suspect has no weapons or other items concealed on him that present a danger to you, him or others.

You have retained the leather jacket. The suspect also has another store's (MAGGS) carrier bag, containing five T-shirts for which there is no receipt. You take possession of these items. It may be necessary for you to arrest the suspect later in respect of these additional items.

PNC person check reports person recorded, not wanted and no markers present.

> ❖ 112, 101, 35, 52, 206, 660, 217, 141, 127
>
> 🗀 1A1, 1A4, 2C1, 2C3, 2I1, 4C1, 4G2
>
> **Note: Behaviours, 🗀1A4, 4C1 and ❖141 should be covered in most circumstances as normal working practices.**

ACTION TO BE TAKEN

What do you know?

◆ The suspect is now in your custody and you are responsible for his safety and welfare in transferring him to the police station until he has been accepted by the Custody Officer. You also need to be aware of your own personal safety and your colleagues'.

◆ You have taken possession of the jacket and T-shirts as you believe them to be stolen property.

What do you need to know?

◆ After your transport has arrived and the arrested person has been conveyed to the police station, you need to make a note of the time of your arrival at the station as the Custody Officer will ask you for this information.

What next?

You are now ready to take the arrested person through to the Custody Officer.

The Custody Officer has responsibility for making sure that there are grounds to authorise the detention of the arrested person. The Custody Officer will want to know if you have searched the person, and may require a further search to be carried out.

You need to be able to give enough information to the Custody Officer for him/her to be able to authorise the person's detention, and also make him aware of any relevant information concerning the person's health and welfare.

Having already decided that that the arrest was necessary and that you had reasonable grounds to suspect the person of stealing the jacket, you need to tell the Custody Officer this.

You need to give the Custody Officer the following information:

- the time and place of the arrest;

- the details of the offence that gave you your reasonable suspicion and grounds for the arrest (e.g. what the store detective said, necessity test areas);

- as per the necessity test, explain that the arrest is necessary to investigate the offence in a prompt and effective manner;

- what property you have taken into your possession and its location;

- your time of arrival at the police station with the arrested suspect; and

- if any significant statement was made.

The Custody Officer has to decide whether there are sufficient grounds and reasons to authorise the arrested person's detention at the police station. If detention is authorised, it is the Custody Officer's responsibility to ensure that the detainee is fit to be detained and interviewed. Detention will usually be authorised for the purposes of preserving and securing evidence, and to obtain evidence by way of questioning. This requires you to obtain and record the necessary evidence, e.g. your pocket notebook, the store detective's statement and recording of property in the relevant register. You will be required to carry out these tasks immediately, as the detainee must be interviewed as soon as practicable.

Having had his detention authorised, Jake Rowlands is informed of his rights. These include the right to free independent legal advice, which on this occasion is declined. The detainee is then searched and found to be in possession of £5.95 cash and two keys on a ring. These will be seized and placed into a property safe until he is released when they will be returned.

You will now be required to complete a pocket notebook entry in accordance with your own force guidelines. An example of this could be as follows.

14:30   Call received to attend Nixon's department store. Adult male shoplifter.

14:35   Nixon's department store, Union Street.

Where I attended the security office and saw Maria Whatley, the store detective, in company with a man who I believe to be Jake ROWLANDS. I said to ROWLANDS, 'Listen to what the store detective has to say.' Maria Whatley then said, in the presence and hearing of the suspect, 'I saw this man in the men's wear department, where he removed a leather jacket (indicating exhibit MEW 1) from its hanger, put it on and then left the store making no attempt to pay. Outside the store, I challenged him and asked him to accompany me back to the security office.' ROWLANDS shrugged.

14:40   I then said to ROWLANDS, 'You have heard what the store detective has had to say. I am arresting you on suspicion of theft of the jacket. You do not have to say anything. But it may harm your defence if you do not mention when questioned something which you later rely on in Court. Anything you do say may be given in evidence.'

ROWLANDS made no reply.

I then took possession of the brown leather jacket (Exhibit MEW/1). I also took possession of a Maggs' carrier bag containing five T-shirts (Exhibit PCS3112/1), each labelled at £19.99, for which there was no receipt.

Transport requested. ROWLANDS conveyed to Castleton Police Station.

14:50   Castleton Police Station.

Documentation procedure conducted for Jake ROWLANDS, 14.06.1980, Welford Custody Reference CC509/05.

15:05   Pocket book entry completed re arrest of Jake ROWLANDS in Report Writing Room.

What next?

At 15:30 hours Maria Whatley, the store detective, arrives at the station to give a witness statement. This is not your statement but you will be required to write it. This is effectively a witness interview and the principles outlined in Chapter 5 will apply.

It is essential that you ensure the key points are covered. One very important area will be the identification of Rowlands and what Maria Whatley was able to see him doing. These matters are generally covered in the list of identification points in the case of *R v Turnbull*.

The mnemonic ADVOKATE covers these issues:

♦ **A**mount of time the suspect was under observation.

♦ **D**istance between the witness and the suspect.

♦ **V**isibility, i.e. what was the lighting like, what were the weather conditions?

♦ **O**bstructions to the witness's view of the suspect.

♦ **K**nown or seen before, i.e. does the witness know the suspect and, if so, how?

♦ **A**ny reason for remembering the suspect, i.e. if the witness has seen the suspect before?

♦ **T**ime lapse between the first and any subsequent identification to the police.

♦ **E**rrors between the first recorded description of the suspect and his actual appearance.

When obtaining the description of the suspect it is important to avoid leading questions which might imply the answer, such as 'How short was he?' or 'How young did he seem?'. Use open questions, such as 'What age was he?', and ask if the witness can estimate a range (e.g. between 5'10" and 6 feet) rather than giving a precise height.

When describing a person there are ten points to remember to cover the description in full:

♦ colour;

♦ sex;

♦ age;

♦ height;

♦ build;

- hair (style and colour);

- complexion;

- distinguishing features, e.g. tattoos, scars, facial hair, spectacles, etc.;

- clothing (from top to bottom);

- whether carrying anything.

An example of Maria Whatley's statement might read as follows.

RESTRICTED (when complete)

WITNESS STATEMENT
(CJ Act 1967, s 9; MC Act 1980, ss 5A(3) (a) and 5B; MC Rules 1981, r 70)

Statement of: Maria WHATLEY   URN:

Age if under 18:   Over 18   (if over 18 insert 'over 18')   Occupation: Store Detective

---

This statement (consisting of 2 page(s) each signed by me) is true to the best of my knowledge and belief and I make it knowing that, if it is tendered in evidence, I shall be liable to prosecution if I have wilfully stated anything in it, which I know to be false, or do not believe to be true.

Signature: *M Whatley*   Date:

Tick if witness evidence is visually recorded ☐ (supply witness details on rear)

At 14:15 hours on (day and full date) I was on duty in Nixon's Department Store, Union Street, Castleton on the ground floor in the men's wear department. At this time I noticed a man standing by the coats and jackets section. The man was a white male, aged in his mid to late twenties, about 5' 8" in height, with short, spiky, mousey hair and a pale complexion. He was clean shaven and had small steel-framed spectacles. He was wearing a plain black sweatshirt and faded denim jeans, with black trainers with red stripes. He was carrying a green and white 'Maggs' carrier bag. My attention was drawn to the man as he appeared to be looking about the department more than at the clothes he was standing by.

I was watching the man for about three minutes from a distance of about twenty feet as I was standing by the shirts and ties. The lighting in the store is very good and I had a clear and unobstructed view of the man whom I have no recollection of seeing before. I now believe this man to be Jake Rowlands.

I saw the man select a brown leather jacket which he removed from its hanger and tried on whilst still holding onto the carrier bag. He was looking about himself all the time and appeared nervous. I used my mobile phone to contact the security guard who was also on the ground floor.

►

The man placed the empty hanger back on the display rail and then began to walk towards the Union Street exit, passing two tills before leaving the store, having made no attempt to pay for the jacket.

Outside the store, I approached the man in company with the uniformed security guard and said, 'I am a store detective from Nixon's and I have just seen you take the leather jacket you are wearing from a display and leave the store without paying for it. I must ask you to accompany me back to the security office.' The man made no comment and accompanied us back to the security office where the police were contacted. In the security office, I requested the man to remove the jacket which he handed to me. The brown leather jacket was a 'Nixon's' brand and still had the price label for £149.99. I produce this item as exhibit MEW/1.

At 14:35 hours that day Constable 3112 arrived at the security office and said 'Listen to what the store detective has to say.' I then said, in the presence and hearing of the suspect, 'I saw this man in the men's wear department, when he removed a leather jacket (indicating exhibit MEW/1) from its hanger, put it on and then left the store making no attempt to pay. Outside the store, I challenged him and asked him to accompany me back to the security office.'

Rowlands shrugged his shoulders. Constable 3112 then said to Rowlands, 'You have heard what the store detective has had to say. I am arresting you on suspicion of theft of the jacket. You do not have to say anything. But it may harm your defence if you do not mention when questioned something which you later rely on in Court. Anything you do say may be given in evidence.' Rowlands made no reply.

Constable 3112 took possession of the brown leather jacket (exhibit MEW/1). This item is identical in every respect to those sold in my employer's store.

No person has any right or authority to take any of my employer's property. My employer agrees to abide by any decision the police may make regarding this incident.

Signature: *M Whatley*

Signature witnessed by: *(Your signature)*

(Complete example of contact details and inconvenient dates here)

Home address: *C/O NIXON'S DEPARTMENT STORE, UNION STREET, CASTLETON, EASTSHIRE*

Postcode: *CA6 4DR*

Home telephone No. *N/A*

Mobile/Pager No. *N/A*

E-mail address (if applicable and witness wishes to be contacted by e-mail):

mwhatley@nixons.co.uk

Contact point (if different from above): *N/A*

Address: *N/A*

Work telephone No. *0161 2750855*

~~Male~~ / Female (delete as applicable)

Date and place of birth: *30.4.60 COVENTRY*

Maiden name: *WALLACE*

Height: *5' 7"*   Ethnicity Code: *W1*

State dates of witness non-availability: *13–28 August*

I consent to police having access to my medical record(s) in relation to this matter:	Yes ☐	No ☐	N/A ✔
I consent to my medical record in relation to this matter being disclosed to the defence:	Yes ☐	No ☐	N/A ✔
The CPS will pass information about you to the Witness Service so that they can offer help and support, unless you ask them not to. Tick this box to decline their services:	Yes ☐	No ☐	N/A ✔

Does the person making this statement have any special needs if required to attend court and give evidence? (e.g. language difficulties, visually impaired, restricted mobility, etc.) If 'Yes', please enter details.	Yes ☐	No ✔
Does the person making this statement need additional support as a vulnerable or intimidated witness? If 'Yes', please enter details on Form MG2.	Yes ☐	No ✔
Does the person making this statement give their consent to it being disclosed for the purposes of civil proceedings (e.g. child care proceedings)? (No box should be ticked on all three questions in this box.)	Yes ☐	No ✔

Having obtained the statement, you inform the store detective that you will contact her and update her regarding what has happened with the case once you are in a position to do so.

You now continue your investigation.

What do you know?

♦ That a statement has been obtained form the store detective outlining exactly what she saw the defendant do.

♦ The property (jacket) that has allegedly been stolen has been seized and dealt with according to force policy.

What do you need to know?

♦ If the five t-shirts in the 'MAGGS' carrier bag that the suspect had with him are also stolen.

♦ If the suspect has any previous convictions for this type of offence and if he has what the details are.

How are you going to find that out?

◆ Visit MAGGS store and get them to check their stock and/or sales records to ascertain if they sell the t-shirts and if they have sold any t-shirts that day or if any are missing from stock. Most stores can now audit the cash register receipts as most items are coded and they can tell you what item they have sold and when. Also check if there is any CCTV within the store you may be able to gather evidence from and check with the staff who may remember the suspect.

◆ Conduct a PNC person check and obtain a full print out of previous convictions for suspect Jake Rowlands.

What next?

You conduct the above enquiry with MAGGS store. They clarify that the store took payment for five t-shirts the same as those in Rowlands' possession that morning, and there are no others missing from stock. There is no sign of Rowlands on the store CCTV for that morning. Although you are unable to clarify that the t-shirts in his possession have been paid for, you are also unable to prove that they have been stolen. You can therefore conclude this part of the enquiry and the t-shirts can be returned to Rowlands on his release from custody. If the t-shirts had turned out to be stolen then you would need to arrest Rowlands for this further offence before you could ask him questions in interview regarding it or progress the case any further.

The previous convictions check shows that Rowlands has over the last three years obtained five previous convictions for 'dishonesty/theft-related offences', three of those were shoplifting. You outline the circumstances to the duty inspector, who authorises you to perform a search of the suspect's home address using powers under s 18 PACE Act 1984 (see **Appendix 2**), in order to look for stolen property or items used in the commission of an offence.

You perform a search of the premises but do not find or recover any items. You inform the Custody Officer, who endorses this on the custody record and you complete the relevant documentation required in relation to the search carried out, such as search forms, search register, PNB, etc.

Having completed all of the necessary enquiries/investigation, the next stage is to prepare to interview the detainee using the PEACE interviewing model.

P – Planning and preparation

E – Engage and explain

A – Account, clarification and challenge

C – Closure

E – Evaluation

It is important to know the reason for interviewing a suspect. PACE Code C gives a definition of an interview:

> An interview is the questioning of a person regarding his involvement or suspected involvement in a criminal offence or offences which by virtue of paragraph 10.1 of Code C is required to be carried out under caution.

The planning and preparation stage

Having obtained the necessary statements and before interviewing the detainee, it is necessary to prepare an interview plan. This will give you confidence when conducting the interview and ensure that the essential factors are covered.

There are a number of points that you need to consider and include in your interview plan:

♦ What is/are the offence(s) and the 'points to prove'?

♦ What defences might the suspect put forward?

♦ What facts are known?

♦ What information do you need to know?

What is/are the offence(s) and the 'points to prove'?
The offence in this example is theft. Section 1(1) of the Theft Act 1968 states:

> A person is guilty of theft if he dishonestly appropriates property belonging to another with the intention of permanently depriving the other of it.

The key points to prove are:

(a) the suspect acted dishonestly;

(b) the property was appropriated;

(c) the property belonged to another; and

(d) the suspect had the intention of permanently depriving the other of it.

What defences might the suspect put forward?
Having identified the offence and the points to prove, the next thing to consider is what defences the suspect might put forward. In this example, some potential defences could be:

- The suspect did not act dishonestly (e.g., the suspect believed he had a right to the property).

- The suspect had no intention of permanently depriving the owner of the property (was going to give it back).

- Alternatively, the suspect may claim that he is not the person the store detective saw.

What facts are known?

The known facts in this example can be obtained primarily from the witness statement given by Maria Whatley, the store detective. These include what the suspect did and how the suspect committed the crime.

- At 14:15 hours at Nixon's department store, in the ground-floor men's wear department, the store detective saw a man described as a white male, aged in his mid- to late twenties, about 5′ 8″ in height, with short, spiky, mousey hair and a pale complexion. He was clean shaven and had small steel-framed spectacles. He was wearing a plain black sweatshirt and faded denim jeans, with black trainers with red stripes. He was carrying a green and white Maggs carrier bag.

- The man was seen to select a brown leather jacket, which he removed from its hanger and tried on whilst still holding on to the carrier bag.

- The man placed the empty hanger back on the display rail and then began to walk towards the Union Street exit, passing two tills before leaving the store, having made no attempt to pay for the jacket. Security staff detained him.

- In the security office, he was asked to remove the jacket.

- The brown leather jacket is a Nixon's brand and has a price label for £149.99.

- No person has any right or authority to take any property of Nixon's department store.

What information do you need to know?

We have already shown that the points to prove will need to be covered during the interview. In particular, it is necessary to try to establish the suspect's intent.

- What was in the suspect's mind at the time?

- Why did he commit the crime?

Pre-interview disclosure of evidence

If the detainee requested legal advice prior to the interview, it would be necessary for you to decide what information you are prepared to disclose prior to the interview. It may be that you decide to disclose all your information to the suspect's representative at that time. Although there is no requirement for you to do this, it is unlikely that the suspect's representative will advise the suspect to take part in the interview unless there has been some disclosure of at least the broad facts and allegation.

You should now be able to complete an interview plan form.

INTERVIEWEE	CUSTODY RECORD No. or Interview No.	DATE
OFFENCE		
POINTS TO PROVE (e.g. dishonesty, intent, etc.)	DEFENCES (including possible areas of defence)	
PURPOSE (of Interview)		
RELEVANT ISSUES		
FACTS ALREADY ESTABLISHED (e.g. offence occurred at a particular time, suspect was wearing particular clothing. Should include significant statement/silence and those facts which may give rise to a Special Warning.)	FACTS TO BE DETERMINED (e.g. where was interviewee at time of offence?)	
RECORD OF INFORMATION DISCLOSED TO SOLICITOR/LEGAL REPRESENTATIVE		

Arrangements for the interview

There are a number of basic factors which need to be considered and organised before the interview can take place. Some of these are as follows.

• Is the detainee fit to be interviewed? This is a decision that the Custody Officer has to make when he authorises the interview. Factors the Custody Officer will consider include whether the detainee needs an uninterrupted period of rest and whether he has been offered a meal or drink.

• Is an interview room available? Other points to consider include whether there are enough chairs, the layout, and familiarisation with the recording equipment.

• If the detainee has requested the presence of a legal representative, is he or she able to attend?

• Have you obtained the necessary witness statements?

• What do you need to take into the interview with you? This will include sufficient tapes and labels, copies of statements or your interview plan, and any exhibits.

Significant statements

If a significant statement has been made and recorded at some point, it is important to make sure that you a have a copy of exactly what was said, where it was recorded and if the suspect has signed it as a correct account. This statement should be covered during the interview at the relevant point.

Bad character evidence

In certain circumstances, specifically if the suspect is denying their involvement in the offence or stating that they have never been involved in anything like this or have no knowledge of any such thing, then bad character evidence may be used; this is normally used within the interview. If the suspect has previous convictions for similar offences committed in a similar way, then this information can be used in interview to prove their previous character, knowledge, etc. There are restrictions and guidance on how this evidence may be used; if you intend to use it obtain guidance beforehand. When preparing for interview it is important that you have full information regarding the suspect's previous history.

❖   112, 101, 35, 36, 1, 46, 52, 53, 206, 660, 217, 141, 127

📁   1A1, 1A4, 2C1, 2C3, 2I1, 4C1, 2H1, 2K2, 4G2, 2G2, 212, 2K1

Note: Behaviours, 📁1A4, 4C1 and ❖141 should be covered in most circumstances as normal working practices.

Engage and explain

This is the first part of the interview and there is a set procedure to follow to ensure that the Codes of Practice are complied with in respect of interviewing suspects. Additionally, by following the step-by-step instructions on the card in the interview room, you will be ensuring fairness to the interviewee, and this will help to reassure you and to build a rapport.

Having placed the tapes in the machine, you must introduce yourself, state the time, remind the interviewee that he is still under caution, and read out the caution. If the interviewee has not received legal advice, he must again be offered the opportunity to receive it.

It is important to create the right atmosphere. This will include how you address the interviewee, establishing whether he has any immediate needs or concerns, taking an interest in his individual circumstances and, where appropriate, showing empathy.

Account, clarification and challenge

Having covered the formal procedures, you are now ready to obtain the interviewee's account. In order to do this it is important to start by asking an open question. An example of this might be:

♦ 'Tell me everything from when you first came into town today.'

♦ 'What happened from when you left home this morning through to when you were arrested today?'

♦ 'What happened today leading to your arrest?'

Remember to listen carefully to everything the interviewee has to say and do not interrupt. Once you have obtained the interviewee's account, you can then ask questions to clarify points. If the account differs from the accounts in the witness statements, you can then challenge the interviewee by referring to these.

It is important to use your interview plan to ensure that you cover all the points to prove, and that you produce the exhibits when appropriate.

Should a suspect choose to make no reply to any questions or requests throughout the course of the interview, then you must continue with your interview plan. Ensure that you ask all of the questions to cover the points to prove for the offence and put any evidence to the suspect that you originally planned. Do not be put off by the silence – continue with your plan.

It may be that during the interview one of the conditions in relation to the 'special warning rules' occurs; this will normally be when a person refuses to answer or respond to you or a specific question. If this occurs, deliver the warning as per force guidelines and continue with your interview plan (most interview prompt sheets that are kept in interview rooms will have the special warning printed on them for your use; if not, always ensure that you take a copy into interview with you).

Closure

Before closing the interview, summarise what the interviewee has said and be prepared to answer any questions he might have. There are a number of formal aspects that are required for the closure of suspect interviews. These are:

(a) stating the time the interview finishes;

(b) handing a notice to the suspect concerning his right to a copy of the tape (Code E); and

(c) sealing the master tape in the presence of the suspect (Code E).

Evaluation

When reviewing all the evidence and what the interviewee has said in relation to the evidence and points to prove, it may be necessary to revisit witnesses either to obtain additional evidence, or to clarify issues. In this case during the interview Jake Rowlands fully admits the offence.

Having concluded the interview it is now necessary to return the interviewee to the Custody Officer. The Custody Officer will need to be updated as to the progress of the investigation in order to decide on the appropriate course of action, issue of fixed penalty ticket, official caution, charge and bail, bail for CPS advice or no further action.

In this case releasing the person and taking no further action is not appropriate as the offence is complete. As the suspect has previous convictions for similar offences then a caution or fixed penalty ticket are not options. The suspect has fully admitted the offence and the investigation is complete and straightforward, therefore CPS advice is not required. The Custody Officer decides that the suspect is to be charged with the offence of theft and bailed to attend court. You charge the suspect and obtain his fingerprints, photographs and DNA sample; you then complete the charge file and submit an intelligence report regarding the information obtained. At this point you contact Maria Whatley, the store detective, and inform her of the progress of the case.

As outlined in the introduction, shoplifting is an offence that can be committed by a variety of people from different backgrounds. The different circumstances in each case you encounter will direct you as to how to deal with that specific offence. During your career you may find that you use many different methods to deal with the offence of shoplifting.

❖   112, 141, 101, 36, 35, 42, 74, 52, 660, 217, 127, 57, 206

🗀   1A1, 1A4, 4G2, 2C1, 2C3, 2C4, 2I1, 2K2, 4C1, 2A1, 1A2, 1B9, 2J1, 2K1

Behaviours
Respect for race and diversity, team working, community and customer focus, effective communication, problem-solving, personal responsibility, resilience.

Note: Behaviours, 🗀1A4, 4C1 and ❖141 should be covered in most circumstances as normal working practices.

Assessment documentation

A **personal statement** prepared by you would be the most likely format for evidence from this type of scenario. If you had been in company with another officer then a **witness testimony** by them may have been used. The only witness in this case that you have to your actions is the store detective who only actually witnessed part of your duties and therefore could only comment on this small area. The Custody Officer could be a witness to the competencies claimed whilst in the custody area. If an assessor had been with you at the time then they would have submitted an **observation report** outlining the NOS areas that they had awarded competence in.

In this instance you would produce a **personal statement** outlining exactly what you did and highlighting the units, performance criteria, knowledge and range that you wish to claim from this. There may be **witness testimony** from store detective or Custody Officer. The documentation you use will differ from force to force but there will normally be a specific form to be used. If you are unsure, seek advice from your assessor/supervisor prior to submitting it for assessment.

▶

The assessor will need to check that your evidence is acceptable and validate that it actually happened. They can check with a witness for a witness testimony or, if it is a personal statement, they will probably still check with the witness and also be looking at the **other evidence produced (supporting evidence)**, so you must also provide details of this on the personal statement. For this scenario this will be documentation such as:

Incident log ref. no.
Pocket notebook entry (include book and page numbers)
PNC transaction numbers
POFP numbers
Custody record number
Search record number
Interview tape ref. number
Case file number re Rowlands
Intelligence report ref. no.

If an assessor deems it appropriate they may ask **specific questions** regarding certain areas of the evidence for you to answer. These will be recorded, normally in written or voice-recorded format. This is generally done to clarify areas that may not have been fully covered or to look at specific criteria, range or knowledge that have not been achieved by performance. Another method that could be used to achieve this is **professional discussion**; this is similar, only it takes the form of a discussion between the candidate and assessor and is normally covering a greater variety of issues than questioning.

Flowchart – Shoplifting

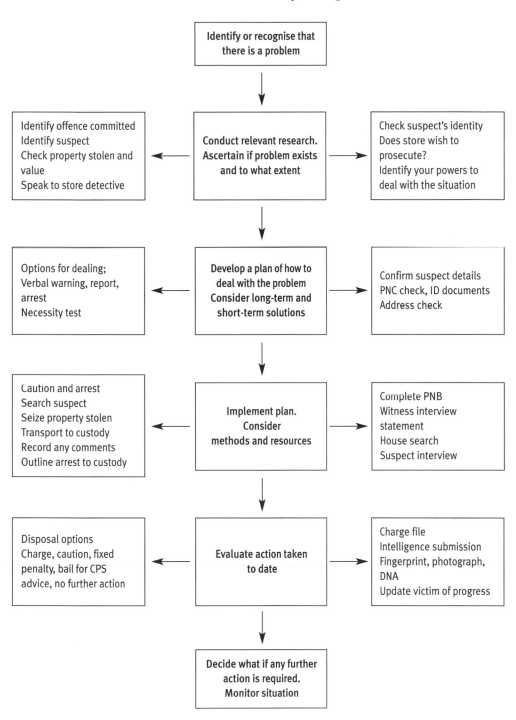

Identify or recognise that there is a problem

↓

| Identify offence committed
Identify suspect
Check property stolen and value
Speak to store detective | ← | **Conduct relevant research.
Ascertain if problem exists and to what extent** | → | Check suspect's identity
Does store wish to prosecute?
Identify your powers to deal with the situation |

↓

| Options for dealing;
Verbal warning, report, arrest
Necessity test | ← | **Develop a plan of how to deal with the problem
Consider long-term and short-term solutions** | → | Confirm suspect details
PNC check, ID documents
Address check |

↓

| Caution and arrest
Search suspect
Seize property stolen
Transport to custody
Record any comments
Outline arrest to custody | ← | **Implement plan.
Consider methods and resources** | → | Complete PNB
Witness interview statement
House search
Suspect interview |

↓

| Disposal options
Charge, caution, fixed penalty, bail for CPS advice, no further action | ← | **Evaluate action taken to date** | → | Charge file
Intelligence submission
Fingerprint, photograph, DNA
Update victim of progress |

↓

**Decide what if any further action is required.
Monitor situation**

Chapter 7
Burglary

This chapter covers criteria within the following units of the National Occupational Standards for student police officers:

Level 3

1A1 – Use police actions in a fair and justified way.
1A4 – Foster people's equality, diversity and rights.
2C1 – Provide an initial police response to incidents.
2C3 – Arrest, detain or report individuals.
2H1 – Interview victims and witnesses
2I1 – Search individuals.
2K2 – Present detained persons to custody.
4C1 – Develop one's own knowledge and practice.
4G2 – Ensure your own actions reduce the risks to health and safety.

Level 4

1B9 – Provide initial support to individuals affected by offending or anti-social behaviour and assess their needs for further support.
2A1 – Gather and submit information that has the potential to support policing objectives.
2G2 – Conduct investigations.
2G4 – Finalise investigations.
2H2 – Interview suspects.
2I2 – Search vehicles, premises and land.
2J1 – Prepare and submit case files.
2K1 – Escort detained persons.

It is likely that the following activities and behaviours from the student officer Role Profile will also be evidenced.

Activities:

112 – Conduct patrol.
41 – Complete prosecution procedures.
141 – Promote equality, diversity and human rights in working practice.
101 – Provide an initial response to incidents.
36 – Conduct custody reception procedures (arresting officer).
35 – Conduct lawful arrest and process procedures.
42 – Prepare and submit case files.
1 – Conduct investigation.
45 – Interview suspects.
46 – Interview victims and witnesses.
74 – Provide care for victims and witnesses.

52 – Search person(s) or personal property.
53 – Search vehicles, premises and land.
660 – Maintain standards for security of information.
217 – Maintain standards of professional practice.
127 – Provide an effective response recognising the needs of all communities.
57 – Use information/intelligence to support policing objectives.
206 – Comply with health and safety legislation.

Behaviours:

Respect for race and diversity
Team working
Community and customer focus
Effective communication
Problem-solving
Personal responsibility
Resilience

Introduction

The offence of burglary is defined by the Theft Act 1968, s 9 (see **Appendix 2**). Although the legislation may appear complex on first reading, it can easily be interpreted.

A person commits burglary if he or she enters a building or part of a building, without the owner's or occupier's permission, with the intention to commit one or more of three acts, namely: theft, grievous bodily harm or unlawful damage. The offence can also be committed if the person enters the building or part of a building, then once inside they formulate the intent to steal or inflict grievous bodily harm.

There are different types of burglary. These include:

Dwelling burglary – This is when a burglary is committed in a place where someone resides, such as a house, flat, etc.

Burglary other – This is when a burglary is committed in a place where no one is residing or the place is not meant for a person to reside in such as a garden shed, factory, etc.

Aggravated burglary – This is when a burglary is committed and the person committing it has with them at the time:

W – Weapon of offence

I – Imitation firearm

F – Firearm

E – Explosive

In this chapter we will be dealing with a dwelling burglary.

IDENTIFY THE PROBLEM

The scenario

It is 18:00 hours on a weekday evening and you are on patrol. You receive a call from the communications centre directing you to attend 4 The Grove, Kingston Park. The occupants have returned from work and have found that the property has been broken into. At this time you are in company with your workplace assessor who is conducting an observation of you.

What do you know?

At 18:00 hours today a call was received, requesting the police attend the scene of a break-in at 4 The Grove.

What do you need to know?

◆ Where is 4 The Grove?

◆ Have the occupants disturbed intruders?

How are you going to find that out?

◆ If you don't know the location yourself, ask the communications operator for directions over the radio.

◆ The communications operator will have spoken with the person reporting the incident, so ask the operator if the occupants have disturbed anyone. This is important, as the offender(s) may still be in the vicinity and prompt action could lead to an early arrest.

What next?

Acknowledge the call and make your way to the address. Communications inform you that there has not been anyone disturbed at the scene.

At 18:20 hours you arrive at 4 The Grove. You inform the communications centre that you have arrived. You are met at the front of the property by the occupant, Mr Tait, who tells you, 'I left home at 7.30 am this morning and made sure that the house was locked. I came home from work and found that the patio door at the back of the house was open.' Jewellery, cash and a Gameboy have been stolen.

RESEARCH THE PROBLEM

What do you know?

♦ Between 07:30 hours and 18:00 hours property was taken from that address.

♦ That at 07:30 hours the house was locked and secure.

♦ That the patio door at the back of the house was open by 18:00 hours and that property is missing.

What do you need to know?

♦ Has an offence been committed?

♦ If so, what offence?

How are you going to find that out?

The information already in your possession indicates that the owner of the property believes that it has been stolen. It appears that a burglary has been committed. An essential element will be establishing whether or not anything has been stolen. You need to be certain of this information before classifying the incident as burglary. In order to do this you must find out if the essential elements of the offence of theft are present. A person commits theft when he or she dishonestly appropriates property belonging to another with the intention of permanently depriving the other of it (Theft Act 1968, s 1; see **Appendix 2**; refer to Chapter 6 on shoplifting).

Mr Tait informs you that the jewellery, cash and Gameboy were his property and that no one had any authority to take them without his permission. You are now satisfied that a crime (theft) has been committed, but more information is required before it can be established that the further offence of burglary has been committed. The constituent parts of the offence were outlined at the start of this chapter. In this case the circumstances are as follows.

- ◆ 4 The Grove is a detached bungalow in a cul-de-sac consisting of 16 dwelling houses. It is clearly a building for the purposes of the Theft Act 1968.

- ◆ The house was locked and secure when Mr Tait left for work at 07:30 hours that day.

- ◆ He tells you that no one else has lawful access to his house or is permitted to take his property from within.

- ◆ The rear patio door is open; there is damage to the lock. Someone has entered the house and removed the property without the permission of the owner.

You are now investigating a burglary.

What next?

Mr Tait is a victim of crime and you must deal sympathetically with him, taking into account any circumstances peculiar to him. (Is he vulnerable? Does he need any immediate assistance to help him deal with the incidents? Is he a repeat victim?)

In this case it emerges that Mr Tait is not a repeat victim, and is not classed as vulnerable. He is a victim and requires support and advice to help him through this experience as and when appropriate. His first concern is that his house is currently insecure, with damage to the patio door lock so it will not close or lock. He would like to get this repaired as soon as possible and certainly before he goes to sleep this evening. You reassure him that this will not be an issue and you will arrange for a crime scene investigator (CSI) to attend as soon as possible so that he can arrange repair.

Although it may seem a little late it is also important to discuss crime prevention. You suggest to Mr Tait that his home may benefit from some security improvements with a few inexpensive options such as door and window locks, security lighting, door alarms, etc. He agrees and you arrange for him to receive further advice and a crime prevention survey by the relevant department in your particular force. A neighbourhood watch scheme is running in the area and you arrange with the co-ordinator to heighten awareness in the area via leaflet drops and crime-ring information, etc.

Following this you reassure him that you will be investigating the offence thoroughly and he will be kept updated of any actions taken or information received.

You need to conduct a professional, competent investigation into this offence.

❖ 112, 101, 74, 46, 217, 141

📁 1A4, 2C1, 4C1, 1B9

Note: Behaviours, 📁 1A4, 4C1 and ❖ 141 should be covered in most circumstances as normal working practices.

DEVELOP A PLAN

What do you know?

◆ A burglary was committed at 4 The Grove between 07:30 hours and 18:00 hours today.

◆ This is a detached bungalow in a cul-de-sac of 16 houses.

◆ Entry was gained by damaging the lock on a patio door at the rear of the house.

◆ Jewellery, cash and a Gameboy were stolen from the property.

What do you need to know?

◆ Is there any forensic evidence left at the scene?

◆ Who committed this offence?

◆ Where is the property? Obtain as much detail as you can that could be used to identify the property (serial numbers, post-coding or unusual marks). Get the owner's manual or guarantee documents if available, as they will have a full description and any photographs that they may have of the property.

It is at this point that you need to confirm the crime to communications and pass them the relevant information to generate a reference number. This may be a crime number or incident number, etc; this will be dependent on the individual force procedure.

The victim will require this number for any dealings that they may have regarding insurance companies or if they wish to contact the police in the future regarding the incident. Procedures will differ between forces but you may need to complete some documentation at this stage such as a crime report or booklet, or a witness statement from the victim. In this case you obtain a victim statement from Mr Tait; remember the procedures regarding victim/witness interviews (as outlined in Chapter 5). As this is a victim statement do not forget to include a victim personal statement (VPS) if the victim wishes to do so; this can be done at a later time if required.

How are you going to find that out?

Your actions at this stage are critical to an effective investigation. You, as the first officer at the incident, are in control of a crime scene containing much valuable information and evidence which may lead to the identification of the offender and the recovery of property.

Think forensic and Crime Scene management. What factors do you need to consider?

The house

- ◆ Has anyone else been in the house recently (other than Mr Tait and the offender(s))?

- ◆ Has any other property been disturbed?

- ◆ Are there any marks inside that were not present before the burglary? Footprints in flowerbeds, damage to surrounding property, etc?

- ◆ The patio door lock – preserve this as best you can. A trained crime scene examiner may be able to obtain crucial evidence from it.

- ◆ Are there any tools or implements in the vicinity that could have been used to force entry to the property? If so, keep them safe for forensic examination. This may involve covering the scene to protect it from the elements.

- ◆ Is there anything left at the scene that was not there before the burglary?

The offender(s)

- ◆ Has anyone been seen in the property?

- ◆ Description of anyone involved?

- ◆ Are you aware of any current intelligence relating to burglaries that may assist in tracing the offender(s)? This could include particular types of modus operandi (methods of committing offences) used by specific criminals in your area.

IMPLEMENT THE PLAN

What next?

It is important to preserve any scene until a forensic examination can take place. Victims of such crimes often wish to tidy the property and clear up any mess caused by the offender. You should explain that it is critical to an effective examination that such evidence is not lost. Check your local force policy on the deployment of crime scene investigators and inform control if you need their specialist services. Try to obtain on ETA for the information of the householder.

Conduct a thorough house-to-house search in the immediate vicinity to see if anyone noticed anything suspicious or out of the ordinary, before or after the event in question.

A search of the garden, neighbouring gardens and the surrounding area should be conducted. This may highlight any property that has been left at the scene or forensic evidence.

On examining the scene you find a large screwdriver on the paving next to the patio door. Mr Tait confirms that it does not belong to him. You also notice a footprint in the soil adjacent to the patio. If possible, leave everything in place until examined by a crime scene investigator. If that is not possible then carefully move the screwdriver to a secure storage space, having first made a note of its exact position. The footprint must be protected – a dustbin lid or plastic bag could be used to cover it. You must give clear advice to the householder regarding the safeguarding of the evidence so as not to contaminate it.

While conducting house-to-house enquiries, you speak to Mrs Andrew of 6 The Grove. She tells you that she saw a man drive a van into the cul-de-sac at 15:00 hours today. She states that she saw the man leave the van outside 4 The Grove and make his way to the rear of the property. She did not see him leave.

Remember you are conducting a witness interview. Follow the guidelines regarding open questions and 5WH as outlined in Chapter 5.

Remember ADVOKATE! Refer to Chapter 6 (shoplifting).

You obtain a detailed description of this man: 6 feet tall, white, slim build with short, dark brown coloured hair, aged approximately 25 years. He was wearing a red rugby-type jersey, blue denim jeans, and white training shoes with three black stripes on the side of each shoe.

- Obtain a witness statement from Mrs Andrew.

- Continue with house-to-house enquiries. There may be more witnesses to this incident.

Mr Black of 15 The Grove tells you that he saw a blue van parked near to 4 The Grove earlier that afternoon as he was watching the TV. He did not see anyone with the vehicle.

Having questioned Mr Black, you now know that he saw a blue Transit-type van. He could remember a partial registration number – PJ51***.

You obtain a witness statement from Mr Black.

ACTION TAKEN

What do you know?

- The description of the man.

- Some detailed information about the vehicle.

- Witness statements in relation to the above.

What do you need to know?

- The identity and whereabouts of the man.

- The identity, owner/registered keeper and location of the vehicle.

How are you going to find that out?

You liaise with and submit your information to the intelligence unit. They have specialist knowledge and expertise in profiling individuals. Intelligence identifies three individuals matching the description provided by the witness. All three have previous convictions for committing dwelling house burglaries; one is known to use vehicles in the process. This individual is known to be Peter Corry, 24 years (b 11.05.19—), of 23 Beech Road, Kingston Park.

You find intelligence that has been submitted by other officers, which states that Corry was seen by them driving a blue Transit van, registration unknown three days ago in the Kingston Park area.

Searches can be made on the Police National Computer (PNC) using partial registration numbers. The records show that there are two blue Transit vans registered within the area with numbers beginning PJ51***, one of which is not currently registered to an owner. The other vehicle is registered to a parcel delivery company, which confirms that its vehicle was not being used in the area at the time of the burglary, when you check this with them.

What next?

Evaluation of your information suggests that Peter Corry may be linked to this offence. Do you have sufficient information to arrest him?

It is clear that burglary has been committed and you now have reasonable grounds to suspect that Peter Corry is guilty of this offence.

Under the necessity test, COP PLAN ID (as outlined in Chapter 4), arrest is necessary to prevent loss of or damage to property and to investigate the offence.

You arrest Peter Corry at his home address and you search his house using your powers under s 18 of the PACE 1984 (see **Appendix 2**). What should you be looking for? Do not forget personal safety issues and a person search under s 32 of PACE 1984 (as per Chapter 4).

* Clothing worn at the time of committing the offence and seen by the witness.

* Footwear worn at the time that could link him with the footprint left at the scene of the burglary.

* Stolen property, namely the jewellery, cash and Gameboy.

* Tools that could have been used to commit the offence.

* The vehicle.

Remember, when seizing property linked to a crime think forensic. Consult your scene-of-crime officer for advice and guidance if in doubt about the forensic value of an item.

You recover a gold ring and a Gameboy from the home address of Peter Corry (again using your s 18 powers). You book the property into POFP via the relevant channel (as outlined in Chapter 6).

> ❖ 112, 101, 35, 1, 46, 74, 52, 53, 206, 660, 217, 141, 127, 57
>
> 🗀 1A1, 1A4, 2C1, 2C3, 2H1, 2I1, 4C1, 4G2, 1B9, 2A1, 2G2, 2I2, 2K1
>
> **Note: Behaviours, 🗀 1A4, 4C1 and ❖ 141 should be covered in most circumstances as normal working practices.**

What next?

Having arrested Peter Corry, you should present him before the Custody Officer and explain the reasons for his arrest. You need to be able to give enough information to the Custody Officer for him/her to be able to authorise the person's detention, and also make him/her aware of any relevant information concerning the person's health and welfare (as per Chapters 4 and 6).

At this point you need to continue your investigation until you are in possession of sufficient information to progress to a suspect interview.

What do you know?

- Peter Corry has been arrested. He has been seen recently driving a blue Transit van by other officers and he has previous convictions for dwelling house burglaries.

- You have two witness statements from neighbours and a victim statement from Mr Tait confirming that a burglary has occurred and describing the property that was stolen.

- You have searched Corry's house and recovered a gold ring and a Gameboy.

- A footprint impression and a screwdriver were found at the scene of the burglary and preserved for examination by CSI. When Corry was arrested he was wearing a pair of white training shoes with black stripes; these fit the description given by a witness and you seize the shoes as evidence of an offence.

What do you need to know?

- What Corry's previous convictions are and the full details – you may need to introduce bad-character evidence.

- If the property recovered by you can be positively identified by the victim.

- If CSI have any further evidence/information regarding the footprint or screwdriver.

How are you going to find that out?

- Conduct a PNC person check and obtain a printout of full previous convictions.

- Arrange for the victim to view the property and ascertain if he can positively identify it as his stolen property.

- Liaise with CSI regarding any progress that may have made with the footprint or screwdriver.

What next?

You obtain a copy of Corry's full previous convictions in preparation for interview. The victim has positively identified the gold ring and Gameboy as those stolen from his home. The gold ring had a small engraving of his grandfather's initials 'ST' on the inside of it and the Gameboy had been marked with a postcode; this made them both easy to identify. A witness statement is obtained from the victim covering this identification.

CSI inform you that they have found a fingerprint on the screwdriver and the shoes that you seized from Corry on arrest may be a match to the footprint found at the scene. They will need to send these away for expert examination before this evidence can be confirmed and cleared as admissible for court.

The next stage is to prepare to interview the detainee using the PEACE interviewing model (as per Chapter 6).

During interview Corry makes no reply to any of the questions put to him. You update the Custody Officer who decides that the most appropriate way forward in these circumstances is to bail Corry to return to the police station in four weeks at a given time and date. This will allow you to receive the results of the forensic examination and seek advice on the case from the CPS.

You complete an advice file and submit any intelligence gained during the investigation via the relevant channels, and you ensure that your PNB is completed.

It is important to keep the victims of crime informed about the progress of the investigation. Mr Tait should be contacted and updated accordingly. It is good practice also to update the other witnesses who assisted with the investigation, as well as to take the opportunity to thank them and explain that their efforts have helped bring an offender to justice. Also point out that should the matter go to court they will still be required as witnesses and you will keep them updated.

❖ 112, 141, 101, 41, 36, 35, 42, 1, 45, 46, 74, 52, 53, 660, 217, 127, 57, 206

🗁 1A1, 1A4, 2C1, 2C3, 2H1, 2I1, 2K2, 4C1, 4G2, 2A1, 1B9, 2G2, 2G4, 2H2, 2I2, 2J1, 2K1

Behaviours
Respect for race and diversity, team working, community and customer focus, effective communication, problem-solving, personal responsibility, resilience.

Note: Behaviours, 🗁1A4, 4C1 and ❖141 should be covered in most circumstances as normal working practices.

Assessment documentation

As your assessor has been performing an observation of you during this scenario then the most likely form of evidence will be an **observation report**; this should be completed by your assessor and will outline the NOS areas that they have awarded competence in.

If you had been in company with another officer then a **witness testimony** by them may have been used. Alternatively if you had been alone you could submit a **personal statement** outlining exactly what you did and highlighting the units, performance criteria, knowledge and range that you wish to claim from this. The documentation that will be used will differ from force to force but there will normally be a specific form to be used. If you are unsure, seek advice from your assessor/supervisor prior to submitting it for assessment.

For an **observation report** the assessor will not need to validate any evidence as they have actually observed it happen. If you had submitted a **personal statement** then the assessor will need to check that your evidence is acceptable and validate that it actually happened. They can check with a witness for a witness testimony or, if it is a personal statement, they will probably still check with the witness and also be looking at the **other evidence produced (supporting evidence)**, so you must also provide details of this on the personal statement. For this scenario this will be documentation such as:

Incident log ref. no /crime ref. no.
Pocket notebook entry (include book and page numbers)
PNC transaction numbers
POFP numbers
Custody record number/Search record number
Interview tape ref. number
Case/advice file number re Corry/forensic report ref. no.
Intelligence report ref. no.
Referral details crime prevention.

If an assessor deems it appropriate they may ask **specific questions** regarding certain areas of the evidence for you to answer, these will be recorded, normally in written or voice-recorded format. This is generally done to clarify areas that may not have been fully covered or to look at specific criteria, range or knowledge that have not been achieved by performance. Another method that could be used to achieve this is **professional discussion**; this is similar, only it takes the form of a discussion between the candidate and assessor and is normally covering a greater variety of issues than questioning.

Flowchart – Burglary

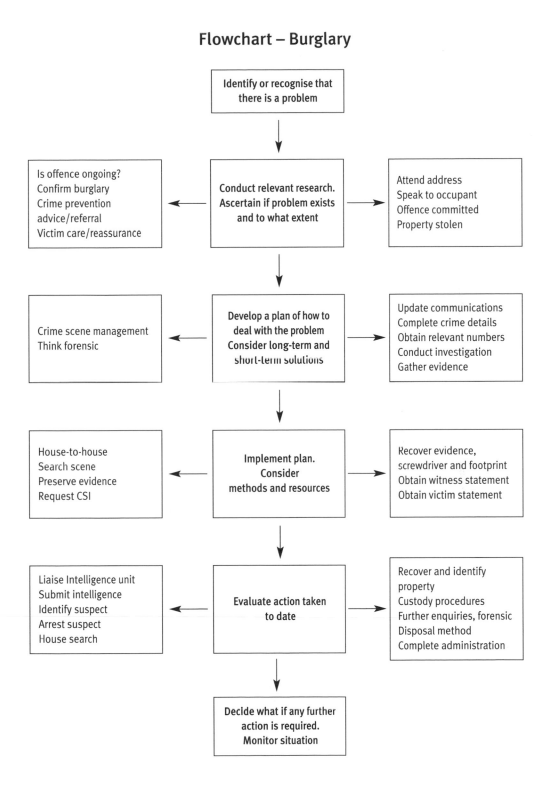

Identify or recognise that there is a problem

↓

Is offence ongoing?
Confirm burglary
Crime prevention
advice/referral
Victim care/reassurance

← **Conduct relevant research. Ascertain if problem exists and to what extent** →

Attend address
Speak to occupant
Offence committed
Property stolen

↓

Crime scene management
Think forensic

← **Develop a plan of how to deal with the problem Consider long-term and short-term solutions** →

Update communications
Complete crime details
Obtain relevant numbers
Conduct investigation
Gather evidence

↓

House-to-house
Search scene
Preserve evidence
Request CSI

← **Implement plan. Consider methods and resources** →

Recover evidence, screwdriver and footprint
Obtain witness statement
Obtain victim statement

↓

Liaise Intelligence unit
Submit intelligence
Identify suspect
Arrest suspect
House search

← **Evaluate action taken to date** →

Recover and identify property
Custody procedures
Further enquiries, forensic
Disposal method
Complete administration

↓

Decide what if any further action is required. Monitor situation

Chapter 8
Domestic Violence

This chapter covers criteria within the following units of the National Occupational Standards for student police officers:

Level 3

1A1 – Use police actions in a fair and justified way.
1A4 – Foster people's equality, diversity and rights.
2C1 – Provide an initial police response to incidents.
2C3 – Arrest, detain or report individuals.
2C4 – Minimise and deal with aggressive and abusive behaviour.
2I1 – Search individuals.
2K2 – Present detained persons to custody.
4C1 – Develop one's own knowledge and practice
4G2 – Ensure your own actions reduce the risks to health and safety.
4G4 – Administer first aid.

Level 4

1B9 – Provide initial support to individuals affected by offending or anti social behaviour and assess their needs for further support.
2A1 – Gather and submit information that has the potential to support policing objectives.
2G2 – Conduct investigations.
2J1 – Prepare and submit case files.
2K1 – Escort detained persons.

It is likely that the following activities and behaviours from the student officer Role Profile will also be evidenced.

Activities:

112 – Conduct patrol.
141 – Promote equality, diversity and human rights in working practice.
101 – Provide an initial response to incidents.
36 – Conduct custody reception procedures (arresting officer).
35 – Conduct lawful arrest and process procedures.
42 – Prepare and submit case files.

1 – Conduct investigation.

74 – Provide care for victims and witnesses

52 – Search person(s) or personal property.

660 – Maintain standards for security of information.

217 – Maintain standards of professional practice.

127 – Provide an effective response recognising the needs of all communities.

57 – Use information/intelligence to support policing objectives.

206 – Comply with health and safety legislation.

207 – Provide first aid.

Behaviours:

Respect for race and diversity

Team working

Community and customer focus

Effective communication

Problem-solving

Personal responsibility

Resilience

Introduction

Domestic violence is a serious problem that has an impact on everyone involved.

Over the last 30 years domestic violence in the UK has gone from being a largely unspoken subject to one which is being tackled and confronted by government and statutory bodies and the voluntary sector. In 1971 Refuge opened the first safe house for women and children experiencing domestic violence. Today there are over 400 refuges nationally and domestic violence receives much greater attention.

What is meant by domestic violence?

Any incident of threatening behaviour, violence or abuse (psychological, physical, sexual, financial or emotional) between adults (18 years or over) who are or have been intimate partners regardless of gender or sexuality. It will include family members, who are defined as mother, father, son, daughter, brother, sister, grandparents, whether they are directly related, in-laws or step-family.

Facts and figures

Although domestic violence is chronically under reported research estimates that it:

◆ accounts for 16% of all violent crime;

◆ has more repeat victims than any other crime (on average there will be 35 assaults before a victim calls the police);

◆ costs in excess of £23 billion a year;

◆ claims the lives of two women each week and 30 men per year;

◆ is the largest cause of morbidity world wide in women aged 19–44, greater than war, cancer or motor vehicle accidents;

◆ will affect 1 in 4 women and 1 in 6 men.

IDENTIFY THE PROBLEM

The scenario

It is 23:15 hours on a Friday night. You are on mobile patrol with a colleague when you receive a call from the communications centre, directing you to attend 47 Carnforth Gardens, Castleshire. BT received an incomplete 999 call from this address. The call was described as being from a woman screaming for help. The handset was replaced before an address was given. BT has obtained the address by tracing the call.

What do you know?

◆ At 23:15 hours today an incomplete telephone call was received from a female caller screaming for help.

◆ The handset was replaced prior to any information being given.

◆ The call has been traced to 47 Carnforth Gardens, Castleshire.

What do you need to know?

◆ Is there any further information?

◆ Is there any information about previous incidents at this address?

◆ What is the location of Carnforth Gardens?

How are you going to find that out?

♦ The communication centre may be able to give some more information.

♦ There may be some historic information relating to 47 Carnforth Gardens on the computerised information system, or from some other officer who is currently on duty.

♦ If you do not know where Carnforth Gardens is, ask the communication centre to give you directions.

What next?

Acknowledge the call and make your way to 47 Carnforth Gardens.

On arrival at the address, inform the communications centre that you have arrived at the scene. It may need this information to update the time it has taken to respond to the call. It also needs to be aware you have arrived at the scene, for reasons to do with your health and safety. It may also have obtained further information about the incident in the time it has taken you to travel to the scene.

The communication centre informs you that there is a history of domestic violence at the property. The last call was six weeks ago, when an arrest was made at the premises for a breach of the peace. The person arrested at that time was Paul Barron, one of the registered occupants of the premises.

At this point you need to consider your personal safety and that of your colleague. Remember the principles outlined in Chapter 4. As communications have a record of the previous incidents at the house and the details of the person arrested, you could ask for a PNC person check on Paul Barron to ascertain if there are any warning markers regarding this individual such as weapons, drugs, violence, etc. It may be a good time for them to check if there are any other persons residing at the address, who they are and how old they are; this may be recorded from the previous incidents. This will give you an idea of whether or not there are children at the address and will help you to build up a picture of what you may be dealing with on arrival.

What next?

You and your partner knock on the door of the premises; a man opens the door and asks you what you want. You say that there has been an incomplete 999 call from this address and that you need to check it out. You ask him if you can enter the premises to check on the well-being of the occupants.

The man says that he has no idea what you are talking about and that nobody has used the telephone that evening.

The man immediately becomes aggressive and refuses to allow you to enter the premises. He states that it is far too late at night, and says that if you return in the morning he will talk to you.

RESEARCH THE PROBLEM

What do you know?

♦ You know there has been an incomplete emergency 999 call which has been traced to this address.

♦ You know the person on the telephone line was female.

♦ You know that the man who has answered the door does not want to give you access to the premises.

♦ You know that he has become aggressive immediately.

What do you need to know?

Are you at the right address; is it possible that you are at the wrong premises?

How are you going to find that out?

You check with the communications centre to verify that the address you have attended is the correct address.

The communications centre confirms that you are at the right address.

What next?

You know that you have to gain entry to the premises to check on the well-being of the occupants. At this time you still may not have any knowledge of how many occupants there are, or who they are. Alternatively, the communication checks may now be complete and you may have an idea of who may be in the house.

What do you need to know?

♦ Do you have any right of entry to the premises?

◆ If so, what are your powers of entry?

◆ Has there been a breach of the peace?

◆ If so, it is your duty to prevent any action likely to result in a breach of the peace in both public and private places.

Under common law a constable may arrest without warrant any person:

(a) who is committing a breach of the peace;

(b) who he or she reasonably believes will commit a breach of the peace in the immediate future; or

(c) who has committed a breach of the peace where it is reasonably believed that a recurrence of the breach of the peace is threatened.

The constable must have a genuine belief that there is a real and imminent risk of a breach of the peace occurring.

You do not have evidence that a breach of the peace is being committed, or has been or will be committed, so what other powers do you have?

You do have concerns for the safety of the woman who made the initial call. Do you know if she is safe and well?

How are you going to find that out?

The only way you are going to ensure the well-being of the female caller is by gaining entry to the premises.

Under s 17(1)(g) of PACE 1984 (see **Appendix 2**), a constable may enter premises for the purpose of saving life or limb, or for preventing serious damage to property. Ensuring the well-being of the female caller would fall within s 17(1)(g).

What next?

You have the power to enter the premises; your next course of action is gaining entry. You again speak to the man at the door. You inform him that you need to speak to the woman who made the phone call; you have to verify that everything is all right with everybody concerned.

You ask the man for his details; at first he refuses to give them to you, but you engage him in conversation, you calm him down by being reasonable, and he starts to talk to you. He gives his name as Paul Barron.

You continue to talk to Barron and inform him that you have the power to enter the premises but you would rather enter at his invitation. Whatever happens, you need to see that the other occupants of the premises are fit and well.

Due to your communication style you have calmed Paul Barron down; he invites you into the premises, so you have not needed to use the powers of entry granted to you under legislation.

Although on this occasion you have not used your powers to enter the property, there will be occasions when you do need to use them. If this occasion had been one of those then again you must consider your own personal safety and that of your colleagues. If this person is going to have to be physically removed in order for you to gain entry then it is highly likely that a breach of the peace may occur. It may be a good idea to request further assistance, as you know that you may have a detainee to deal with as well as who ever may be in the house.

You and your colleague follow Barron into the living room of the premises.

DEVELOP A PLAN

What are your priorities at a possible domestic violence incident once you have secured lawful entry?

Your first priority is to protect all persons from injury. This includes you and your colleague. Generally, in order to ensure this you need to split up the parties involved and take control of the incident. Be careful where you go in the house. For example, it is not good practice to take a potentially aggressive individual into the kitchen. In the kitchen there are many items which may be used as weapons.

You follow Paul Barron into the living room of the premises. A woman is sitting on the settee. She looks as if she has been crying and her hair is dishevelled, but there are no visible injuries. Barron sits beside her, which appears to make her anxious. You ask her for her name, and she tells you that she is Penny Wells. You ask her if she is all right, and she nods and says 'Yes'.

You are not happy about the situation and decide you want to talk to Penny Wells away from Paul Barron. He appears to be trying to intimidate her with his presence. You need to find out if there are other occupants in the house and if they are fit and well.

You ask Penny to come into the hallway to talk to you, and you ask your colleague to talk to Paul. As soon as you try to get Penny by herself, Paul Barron becomes agitated and gets to his feet, stopping Penny from moving.

You need to take control of the situation. You need to investigate what has happened. Penny Wells is obviously not comfortable and appears to be intimidated by Paul Barron.

You inform Paul that you need to speak to Penny by herself and will not leave the premises until you have done so. You ask Penny to go into the hallway, and stand between her and Paul to let her get past.

What are your considerations?

If an assault has taken place prior to your arrival, consider what the offender is likely to do if you are about to take some form of action.

♦ He might become violent and assault Penny Wells, you or your colleague.

♦ If he has committed an offence, he might try to leave the premises.

♦ There might be other persons on the premises whom he could assault or use to assist his escape.

Both you and your colleague need to be very aware of health and safety considerations for everybody involved.

This is where the conflict-management model and impact factors (as outlined in Chapter 4) will be of good use to you.

What next?

You want to talk to Penny but do not want to leave your colleague in a vulnerable position. You get Penny as far away from the living room door as possible, but leave the door slightly open so as to be able to hear if there are any raised voices, or so you could request further assistance if you deem it necessary.

You ask Penny what has happened. At first she says nothing, but when you ask her if she made the phone call she breaks down and says that she has been assaulted by Paul. She tells you that she is terrified of him, but she stays because they have two children and he has threatened to hurt her if she leaves with the children.

Penny shows you her upper arms, which are red and beginning to bruise; she tells you that Paul has been dragging her about by her hair, kicking her in the back and upper legs, and has told her to say nothing to the police. She says that she cannot stand it anymore and she wants to leave with her two children. She tells you that her back and upper thighs are covered in bruises where he has hit and kicked her, but he is careful not to hit her where it shows. She also tells you the assaults have been going on for some time, and that they are getting more frequent and more severe. You ascertain if Penny requires first aid; at this present time she does not. You suggest that in view of her injuries she should visit a doctor the following day to be checked.

What next?

Do you have enough evidence to arrest Paul Barron?

What do you know?

You have seen the bruising on Penny Wells's upper arms and she has informed you that her attacker was Barron. Do you have reasonable suspicion that an offence has been committed?

You have reasonable suspicion that an offence has been committed and under the necessity test, COP PLAN ID (as outlined in Chapter 4), arrest is necessary to prevent injury to that person or others and to investigate the offence.

Officers have discretion within a power of arrest not to use that power for a particular incident, where they believe it is not necessary or proportionate. Every such decision must be justified and documented in the same detailed way as a decision to use the power of arrest, but in domestic violence situations the presumption is towards arrest where lawful, necessary and justifiable.

If you do not arrest an offender at a domestic violence incident:

(a) be prepared to justify your decision;

(b) make a detailed written record as to why you have not arrested;

(c) explain the reason to the victim;

(d) reassure the victim that every step will be taken to –

    (i) prevent a recurrence;

    (ii) offer help, advice and protection.

Police services run a positive action policy in relation to domestic violence. Arrest would normally be the appropriate form of action wherever the power exists.

You can arrest without a complaint from the victim provided you have evidence of an offence and reasonable grounds to believe that the alleged offender is responsible.

> ❖ 112, 101, 1, 206, 660, 217, 141, 207
>
> 🗀 1A1, 1A4, 2C1, 2C4, 4C1, 4G2, 4G4, 1B9, 2G2
>
> **Note: Behaviours, 🗀 1A4, 4C1 and ❖ 141 should be covered in most circumstances as normal working practices.**

IMPLEMENT THE PLAN

What do you need to know?

What offence could you consider?

> There appears to have been an assault on Penny Wells. You are unable to verify the extent of her injuries at the present time, but the assault could range from:
>
> (i) common assault/battery (Criminal Justice Act 1988, s 39); to
>
> (ii) assault occasioning actual bodily harm (Offences Against the Person Act 1861, s 47); to
>
> (iii) wounding or inflicting grievous bodily harm (Offences Against the Person Act 1861, s 20); to
>
> (iv) wounding or causing grievous bodily harm with intent (Offences Against the Person Act 1861, s18).

You decide you have a reasonable suspicion that the offence of assault occasioning actual bodily harm has occurred. You make the decision to arrest Barron.

What next?

You return to the living room where your colleague is still talking to Barron, who appears to be very agitated.

What are your main considerations?

You must be very aware of health and safety. If Barron becomes aggressive, is there anything he could use to hurt anyone in the house? You are aware that there are two children in the house: Where are they? Could Barron gain access to them or to Penny Wells?

You caution Barron and inform him of the grounds of his arrest – that you are arresting him on suspicion of committing assault occasioning actual bodily harm (Offences Against the Person Act 1861, s 47; see **Appendix 2**). Barron immediately tries to get past you to reach Penny Wells. You and your colleague restrain him and, using reasonable force, handcuff him for the journey to the police station.

You will need to make a note of the time of arrest and the reply given by Barron when he was cautioned, if he made any reply. In this case, he did not reply. The Custody Officer will require this information.

What next?

Get Penny out of the way of Barron; if possible get her to go upstairs to the children. Reassure her that you will be back to see her as soon as you have dealt with Barron.

If there are any other officers at the scene you could ask them to remain with Penny and if possible arrange for a friend, family member, neighbour, etc., to stay with her until your return. If there is not another officer at the scene you could request for an officer to attend via communications – this will obviously depend on availability.

The suspect is now in your care and custody. Under s 32 of PACE 1984 (see **Appendix 2**).

You search Barron and are satisfied that he has no weapons or other items concealed on him which present a danger to you or to others.

Your prisoner needs to be transported to the police station as soon as possible.

You contact the communications centre and ask if another officer could attend the address. You briefly outline the circumstances of the situation and of the arrest to the communications centre.

An officer is on duty nearby and will attend the premises within five minutes.

You quickly inform Penny Wells that an officer is en route and will be with her within five minutes, and that you will take Barron to the police station and then return to see her. You check she is all right with this and that she is physically well and does not require any medical treatment. You briefly see the children, a boy of about 3 and a girl of about 5 – both appear to be unharmed. Penny informs you that Barron has never harmed the children.

ACTION TAKEN

What do you know?

The suspect is in your custody. You are responsible for his safety and welfare in transferring him to the police station, until he has been accepted by the Custody Officer at the police station.

What do you need to know?

◆ On arrival at the police station you need to make a note of the time. The Custody Officer will ask for this information.

◆ You need to get full details from the arrested person. You know that his name is Paul Barron, but is that his full name? You need his date and place of birth, and to make a note of any distinguishing marks (such as scars or tattoos), which will ensure that the arrested person has been correctly identified.

◆ You need to know if the arrested person has shown any warning signs, such as illness, self-harm or violence, both for his well-being and for that of the officers at the police station. You may have already checked this previously.

How are you going to find that out?

◆ Conduct a PNC person check.

What next?

You are now ready to take the arrested person through to the Custody Officer.

What do you know?

◆ It is the Custody Officer's responsibility to ensure that there are grounds to authorise the detention of the arrested person.

◆ The Custody Officer will want to know if you have searched the person. He will want a further search to be made, and at this time any articles which could be used to injure or damage the arrested person, any other person or property will be removed. This will include belts, laces and any other items of clothing that could be used to cause injury or damage.

◆ At this time you must be aware of cultural differences. If, for example, a person from the Sikh faith was arrested and his turban had to be removed for health and safety reasons, that person must be supplied with an alternative head covering whilst he is in custody. His turban must also be treated with respect and be stored in a clean place.

What do you need to know?

◆ You need to be able to give enough information to the Custody Officer for her/him to make a decision as to whether to authorise the detention of the arrested person.

◆ He/she also needs to be informed about any injuries or possible illnesses from which the arrested person may be suffering.

How are you going to find that out?

Having decided at the scene of the incident that the arrest was necessary and that you had reasonable grounds for suspecting that the person had committed the offence of s 47 assault, you need to give this information to the Custody Officer. The Custody Officer requires as much detail as possible in order to make an informed decision as to whether to authorise detention. The restriction of someone's liberty is a serious matter, and it is a decision which must not be taken lightly.

What next?

From the information you have supplied the Custody Officer has decided there are sufficient grounds and reasons to authorise the arrested person's detention at the police station.

Having had his detention authorised by the Custody Officer, Paul Barron is informed of his rights. He is offered access to free independent legal advice, which at this time he declines. He is informed that if at any time he wishes to have free independent legal advice, it will be arranged for him. He is then searched and, as mentioned above, property is removed from him.

What do you need to know?

◆ Once the detention procedure is complete you need to obtain further information about the offence.

◆ You need to inform the Custody Officer about your future actions as he/she needs to be aware of what is happening in relation to persons who are in custody.

How are you going to find that out?

You need to return to 47 Carnforth Gardens to see Penny Wells. You need to do this for several reasons:

(a) to continue the investigation;

(b) to reassure Penny that she is safe as Paul Barron is in custody;

(c) to verify the extent of her injuries and to check on the welfare of the children.

What next?

On your arrival at 47 Carnforth Gardens you speak to your colleague, who informs you that Penny Wells has extensive bruising to her upper thighs and back. Penny also states that she is terrified of Barron returning now that she has made a complaint against him.

What are your considerations?

You have to investigate the crime that has been committed, but you must be mindful of the traumatic effect that domestic violence has upon victims and their families. It is particularly important to deal with victims sensitively and professionally.

Professionalism blends effective investigation of the facts with empathy and respect for those involved, to ensure that a positive relationship is established and maintained. One bad experience may make people reluctant to report any further incidents and undermines trust.

It is at this point that you need to provide reassurance to the victim and any witnesses. There are now many agencies that can help victims of domestic violence and their families. These can be housing associations, counselling services, 24-hour free telephone helpline, refuge accommodation, victim support, legal services, medical staff and many voluntary organisations. This needs to be clearly communicated to the victim, bearing in mind the emotional state the person is likely to be in. Citizens Advice Bureau is willing to act as a go-between for victims of domestic violence and has access to a great deal of information, which can assist victims in need of advice. Their service is confidential and this should be outlined to the victim.

As well as the criminal route the victim could also seek protection from the County court (civil action), which may be able to obtain a domestic injunction/order.

> ❖ 112, 101, 36, 35, 1, 74, 52, 206, 660, 217, 141, 127, 207
>
> 🗀 1A1, 1A4, 2C1, 2C3, 2C4, 2I1, 2K2, 4C1, 4G2, 4G4, 1B9, 2G2, 2K1
>
> **Note: Behaviours, 🗀 11A4, 4C1 and ❖ 141 should be covered in most circumstances as normal working practices.**

What do you need to know?

◆ You need to know the details of the assault and, if possible, ascertain the severity of the injuries. This will have a bearing on what offence the offender will be charged with.

◆ You need to obtain statements from the injured person and any other witnesses to the assault. In this case the only witness is Penny Wells. The children did not see the assault.

How are you going to find that out?

You should always consider enhanced evidence gathering. For enhanced evidence gathering you should consider:

◆ speaking to neighbours, friends or (in some cases) work colleagues;

◆ speaking to any other potential witnesses;

◆ preserving 999 tapes;

◆ if applicable, preserving any CCTV footage;

◆ preserving forensic evidence;

◆ interviewing children in the household. You must comply with the document 'Achieving best evidence in criminal proceedings' in relation to interviewing children. Always bear in mind that the welfare of the children is paramount;

◆ photographic evidence – cameras are now available in most forces to gather evidence at the scene;

◆ making use of any call recording, intelligence systems or crime recording systems your force may have. Check for any previous incidents, bail conditions, injunctions or restraining orders;

◆ if applicable, arranging a medical examination of the victim. In some cases it is advisable also to have the offender medically examined.

All the above are obviously dependent on the nature of the offence you are investigating and on the sensitivities of the investigation.

What next?

Statements should be obtained as soon as practicable after the event, when the witness will be best able to recall the incident. You must always be aware, however, of the well-being of the victim. It is now 00:50 hours and Penny Wells has been waiting for your return. She is terrified that Paul Barron will return and hurt her now that she has informed the police of the assault. She tells you she is not going to remain in the house with the children. She also says that she wants to give her statement to the officer who is with her now rather than to you, as they have built up a rapport.

What are your considerations?
You need to investigate this offence and obtain the necessary information to put before the court, but you also need to look to the welfare of the victim and her children.

In practical terms, will the victim be able to concentrate on giving a full statement whilst she is thinking of the welfare of her children and herself, and whilst she is still at the address where she was assaulted?

What do you know?

♦ You know that there has been an assault and a history of domestic violence and that the victim is concerned for her and her children's future safety.

♦ You know the person responsible for the assault is in custody, but you do not know how long he will remain in custody. You do know that he will not be released until the following morning at the earliest.

♦ You know that you require a statement of evidence from the victim and that she would like the other officer to take that statement.

What do you need to know?

Where can Penny Wells and her children stay? Have they some family member they can go to, or will they require assistance from the social services housing association or a women's refuge organisation?

It should be explained to Penny that Barron will not be returning to the house as he is in custody and will remain there until at least lunchtime the following day. Historically, victims of domestic violence were actively encouraged by the police to leave the home address and go to a place of safety as soon as possible. Now with improved legislation and procedures designed to protect the victim, there is no immediate requirement to move the victim and/or any children involved, unless the other party is not in custody or there are other risks apparent such as hostile family, friends, etc. If there are circumstances when you need to sort out urgent accommodation for a victim, communications will normally arrange this on your behalf.

As this is not the case for Penny she decides not to disturb/distress the children by waking them and moving elsewhere that night. Although she feels that she will apply for an injunction as soon as possible, she would feel happier sorting out alternative accommodation for her and the children in the meantime.

How are you going to find that out?

You speak to Penny about future accommodation for her and the children. Penny informs you that her parents live nearby. She would be welcomed there with the children, and she would be safe as Barron would not touch her whilst she was there. The only reason she had not gone before was that each time Barron assaulted her he promised it would be the last time. She is determined now to make a break from Barron for the sake of the children.

What next?

Penny phones her parents, and her father agrees to come round immediately to stay the night with her and the children. As previously mentioned, a statement is required from Penny about the current assault and any prior assaults. Your colleague has built up a rapport with Penny Wells, and to continue this will stay with Penny until her father arrives. The officer will also arrange an appointment to see Penny as soon as possible (the same day) in order to obtain a witness statement from her. You explain to Penny that Barron is in custody and that you are returning to see the Custody Officer to arrange to have Barron detained for court in the morning. It is important not to make any false promises or mislead the victim, so you make it clear that although this is the desired outcome, it depends on numerous factors and may not happen. You say that you will update Penny at all times. In this case you are lucky – the officer will be on duty the following day. It may be that this is not possible, and it would then have to be explained to Penny.

It may be the case that another officer attends the following day, in order to obtain the victim statement and victim personal statement (VPS); it may even be someone from a specialist department (domestic violence unit), dependent on individual force procedures.

There are certain documents that must be completed as soon as possible when dealing with domestic violence, and in these circumstances now would be the appropriate time for you to complete these. You will need to complete a 'report of domestic violence/incident form'. This will cover information such as:

◆ time and date of complaint;

◆ any reference numbers for crimes/incidents, etc.;

◆ full details of victim;

◆ full details of any other people involved/present;

◆ full details of any children, and if there are any concerns for them;

◆ full details/summary of incident;

◆ risk identification for reoccurrence of situation;

◆ details of any actions taken or not taken and reasons why.

This form will be forwarded to a domestic violence co-ordinator who will arrange for details to be input onto a computerised system which enables multi-agency sharing of the information. They will then further risk-assess the actions taken and liaise with the victim and any other agencies if they decide anything further is required.

If a level of risk is identified then a raised level of intervention may be required; force procedures may differ in relation to this and officers should refer to the relevant force domestic violence policy for guidance. This may involve things like crime-prevention surveys at the address and installing window/door locks, alarms or increasing the response level with communications should any calls be received. On most occasions a supervisor will authorise the intervention level.

Should an officer have any concerns regarding the health, care, welfare, etc., of any children at the premises then they should submit a 'juvenile concern (child protect) form'. This should outline full details of the children, the incident and what the concerns are, this will be forwarded to the relevant child-protection department for information and attention.

As a crime (assault) has been committed you will need to obtain full details to update communications and confirm the crime. You may need to complete a crime form. Whilst you are doing this, obtain consent from the victim/injured person for you to obtain a statement/evidence of any medical opinion or treatment received regarding their injuries. This normally takes the form of a statement from the doctor that examined/treated the victim. Again, force procedures may differ in relation to how record this consent. In some cases it may be a specific form or it may be incorporated into another document such as the crime form or domestic violence form.

What next?

The welfare of the victim and her children has been taken care of for the moment and you have completed the documentation you need.

You are now ready to progress how you are going to deal with Barron. On return to custody you liaise with the Custody Officer, who informs you that Barron is now asleep and in these circumstances is entitled to a period of uninterrupted sleep, therefore he will not be available for interview during your tour of duty.

As this is a domestic incident that has resulted in an offence of assault occasioning actual bodily harm, once as much evidence as possible has been obtained then advice from the CPS must be sought in relation to what action should be taken against Barron. This may be:

- ◆ charge and bail with police bail conditions;

- ◆ charge and bail without conditions;

- ◆ bail for further evidence/enquiries to be conducted;

- ◆ charge and put before the first available court to obtain a remand in custody or court-imposed bail conditions.

As you will be going off duty prior to Barron being dealt with, you will need to complete a package of all the evidence, documentation and actions taken so far, in order for other officers to continue the investigation. You may find that this is a regular occurrence, particularly when you are night duty.

The package that you leave may vary in content depending on different procedures but the basics will remain similar. There will need to be enough information left for the investigating officer to continue an efficient and effective investigation. The package may contain the following:

- ◆ incident and crime ref. number/copies of relevant documents;

- ◆ domestic violence form ref. number/copy;

- ◆ medical evidence consent;

- ◆ PNC printout for Barron, previous convictions, etc.;

- ◆ reference numbers for any CSI/forensic evidence or photographs;

- witness statements from officers attending the scene;

- custody record details;

- summary of evidence regarding what has happened so far, what action has been taken, what still needs to be done and any relevant/helpful information for the officers taking over the investigation.

When you return to duty the following night you check on the case progress and find that Barron was charged with assault (sec. 47). He was put before the court where bail conditions to live at a specified address, report to the police station once per week at 7 pm on Tuesdays and not to contact the victim directly or indirectly were imposed on him.

What next?

Once the file of evidence/package is as complete as possible, you should liaise with the Custody Officer and duty supervisor for them to check the contents and brief the next shift.

In order to give the best support, the police service must maintain regular contact with victims or witnesses to keep them informed about developments within the case such as bail dates, the location of the offender and details of court appearances. In some cases this will be the responsibility of the officer in charge of the case; in others it will fall to specialist departments.

As with many policing incidents, the incidents of domestic violence that you deal with will all be different. You need to be prepared to face many and varied situations: in some cases both parties may be drunk, under the influence of drugs, violent, etc. It is also quite common for the person who is the victim to turn on police officers and even attack them as they deal with the offender. When attending domestic incidents officers should be aware of their own and their colleagues' personal safety at all times.

Although circumstances may differ, the basic evidence gathering and investigative process will remain similar to those outlined in the scenario.

❖ 112, 141, 101, 36, 35, 42, 1, 74, 52, 660, 217, 127, 57, 206, 207

🗁 1A1, 1A4, 2C1, 2C3, 2C4, 2I1, 2K2, 4C1, 4G2, 4G4, 2A1, 1B9, 2G2, 2J1, 2K1

Behaviours
Respect for race and diversity, team working, community and customer focus, effective communication, problem-solving, personal responsibility, resilience.

Note: Behaviours, 🗁1A4, 4C1 and ❖141 should be covered in most circumstances as normal working practices.

Assessment documentation

As you were in company with another officer then a **witness testimony** from that officer would be a good format for evidence from this type of scenario. (Remember that the officer will need to be competent them-selves, preferably not a student officer, and you will not be able to claim for any actions that your colleague took.) Remember that the Custody Officer can also be used as a witness in relation to the custody-based NOS. A **personal statement** prepared by you would also be an acceptable format for evidence from this type of scenario. If an assessor had been with you at the time then they would have submitted an **observation report** outlining the NOS areas that they had awarded competence in.

If in this instance you did produce a **personal statement** outline exactly what you did and highlight the units, performance criteria, knowledge and range that you wish to claim from this. The documentation you use will differ from force to force but there will normally be a specific form to be used. If you are unsure, seek advice from your assessor/supervisor prior to submitting it for assessment.

The assessor will need to check that your evidence is acceptable and vali-date that it actually happened. They can check with a witness for a witness testimony or, if it is a personal statement, they will probably still check with the witness and also be looking at the **other evidence produced (sup-porting evidence)**, so you must also provide details of this on the personal statement. For this scenario this will be documentation such as:

Incident log ref. no.
Pocket notebook entry (include book and page numbers) you and other officers
PNC transaction numbers
Crime ref. no.

Domestic violence form ref. no.
Custody record numbers
Any forensic/CSI evidence gathered or photographs taken ref. no.
Intelligence report ref. no.
Overnight package including officer statements, etc., copy or ref. no.
Referral details re any action taken for victim.

If an assessor deems it appropriate they may ask **specific questions** regarding certain areas of the evidence for you to answer, these will be recorded, normally in written or voice-recorded format. This is generally done to clarify areas that may not have been fully covered or to look at specific criteria, range or knowledge that have not been achieved by performance. Another method that could be used to achieve this is **professional discussion**; this is similar, only it takes the form of a discussion between the candidate and assessor and is normally covering a greater variety of issues than questioning.

Flowchart – Domestic Violence

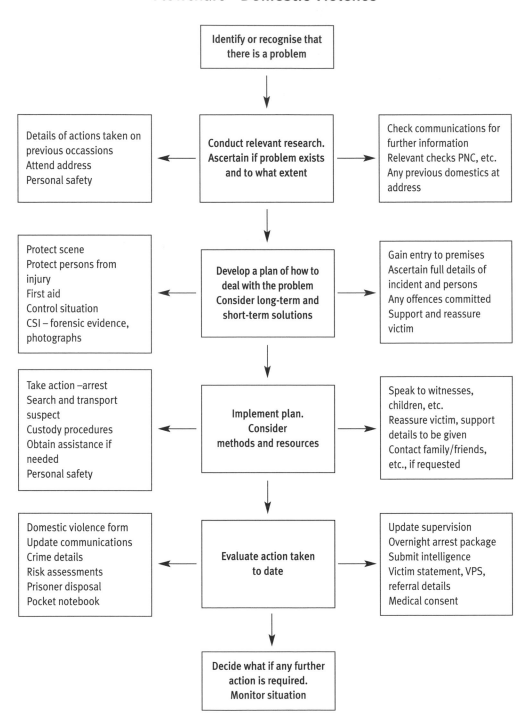

Identify or recognise that there is a problem

Details of actions taken on previous occassions
Attend address
Personal safety

Conduct relevant research. Ascertain if problem exists and to what extent

Check communications for further information
Relevant checks PNC, etc.
Any previous domestics at address

Protect scene
Protect persons from injury
First aid
Control situation
CSI – forensic evidence, photographs

Develop a plan of how to deal with the problem
Consider long-term and short-term solutions

Gain entry to premises
Ascertain full details of incident and persons
Any offences committed
Support and reassure victim

Take action –arrest
Search and transport suspect
Custody procedures
Obtain assistance if needed
Personal safety

Implement plan.
Consider methods and resources

Speak to witnesses, children, etc.
Reassure victim, support details to be given
Contact family/friends, etc., if requested

Domestic violence form
Update communications
Crime details
Risk assessments
Prisoner disposal
Pocket notebook

Evaluate action taken to date

Update supervision
Overnight arrest package
Submit intelligence
Victim statement, VPS, referral details
Medical consent

Decide what if any further action is required.
Monitor situation

Appendix 1
Role Profile
Student Police Officer

Core Responsibilities	Activity no.	Activities The role holder should effectively deliver these key requirements
Community Safety	112	**Conduct patrol** Conduct patrol responding to calls and requests for assistance, countering criminal activity and public disorder and minimising risks to public safety. Effective performance • Determine patrol priorities/activities taking into consideration your briefing, relevant criminal intelligence, policing objectives, and your understanding of local community issues. Make sure that you are properly prepared and equipped to patrol. • Carry out your patrol activities, demonstrating awareness of safety issues at all times. Identify and prevent risks to public safety. Identify potential public disorder and take appropriate actions. Exercise your police powers within the legislation and in accordance with organisational policy and procedures taking into account human rights and diversity issues. • Interact with people in the community, communicate effectively and provide appropriate help and support. Liaise with other agencies. • Respond promptly to requests for police assistance. Keep the control room informed of your location, activities/availability. Request additional resources when needed, identify and inform the supervisor of any issues needing their intervention. • Adopt a problem-solving approach to situations encountered whilst patrolling • On completion of patrol, contribute to debriefing, pass on any intelligence to the relevant individual(s)/agencies. Use all patrol-related equipment correctly in accordance with organisational instructions.
National Occupational Standards		
1A1 – Use police actions in a fair and justified way		2C1 – Provide an initial response to incidents
2C4 – Minimise and deal with aggressive and abusive behaviour		

Core Responsibilities	Activity no.	Activities The role holder should effectively deliver these key requirements
Intelligence	57	**Use intelligence to support policing objectives** Use intelligence to support the achievement of community safety and crime-reduction objectives. Ensure that intelligence is used ethically and in accordance with the relevant legislation, policy protocols and codes and practice. Effective performance • Ensure you are up to date with information and intelligence relevant to your role/duties and that you act in accordance with national intelligence model (NIM). • Make sure other agencies are updated as appropriate. • Target duties to making the best use of available information/intelligence and act on this in accordance with the priority it has been given. • Further develop intelligence in line with local requirements with the purpose of preventing, reducing and detecting crime.
National Occupational Standards		
2A1 – Gather and submit information that has the potential to support policing objectives		
Police operations	69	**Prepare for, and participate in, planned policing operations** Participate in police and agency-led operations, working within appropriate authority limits and carrying out tasks necessary for the successful implementation of the operation whilst managing risks to the operation and acting in accordance with legislation and procedure. Effective performance • Ensure that you are fully briefed regarding the plan and your role within the operation. • Ensure that you have the necessary resources, equipment and authority level to fulfil your role during the operation. Maintain a written record of equipment used in accordance with policy. • Take up position and ensure your actions are co-ordinated with other aspects of the operation as planned. Carry out allocated tasks as per briefing, ensure you comply with relevant legislation and policy. Inform officer in charge of developments during the operation. Take appropriate action within specified guidelines. Use approved information gathering techniques/equipment in accordance with legislation and policy. • Work closely with other internal/external agencies supporting the operation, ensure duty of care to their staff. When participating in other agency-led operations ensure that you carry out the tasks required with integrity in accordance with legislation and policy. • Maintain awareness of potential/actual risks to your own health, safety and welfare. Take action to eliminate risks and to maintain operational integrity. • Maintain a record of your actions throughout the operation as required. Attend debrief to identify good practice and areas for development.

Core Responsibilities	Activity no.	Activities The role holder should effectively deliver these key requirements
Police operations	101	**Provide an initial response to incidents** Respond promptly and take control of the incident by correctly identifying the nature of incident and take appropriate action to ensure that it is dealt with and recorded correctly. Effective performance • Where possible attend the incident within specified Charter Standard response times. Accurately identify the nature of the incident. Record crime details accurately, obtaining relevant information such as first accounts, descriptions of suspects, vehicles and objects. Update the control room. • Take immediate action in line with the nature of the incident. Follow procedures for the type of incident, prioritise your actions. Recognise where an incident is hate crime and respond accordingly. • Consider your safety and that of others at the scene. Direct people positively to a place of safety. Act to prevent other police staff from coming into danger areas. Attend to casualties at the scene, take account of personal safety, providing first aid where appropriate. • Assess and secure the scene taking into account cross-contamination. Secure and preserve evidence. • Give basic scene preservation advice. • Assess the facts. Establish if immediate response is required, request dispatch of the appropriate resources, e.g. police, fire service, ambulance. Provide updates to the control room/supervisors including information on the location, casualties, hazards, access routes and emergency services present and required. Request further resources if needed. • Provide adequate advice/support to victims and witnesses, explain legal and procedural processes. Communicate sensitively and take into account community and diversity issues. • Accurately complete all incident-related documentation and submit for supervision within agreed timescales. Inform and update other staff as appropriate. • When dealing with a major incident, assume interim command until relieved by a more senior officer and liaise closely with other emergency services and agencies present. • Maintain an accurate record of all decisions and subsequent action taken.
National Occupational Standards		
2C2 – Prepare for, and participate in, planned policing operations		2C1 – Provide an initial response to incidents

Core Responsibilities	Activity no.	Activities The role holder should effectively deliver these key requirements
Investigation	1	**Conduct initial investigation** Conduct the initial investigation and scene preservation in accordance with the relevant investigation policies and legal requirements, demonstrating support for victims and witnesses and recognising any possible impact on the community. Effective performance • Determine the nature of the incident, establish whether an offence has been committed, and carry out an initial risk assessment. Gather and retain available material in a retrievable format, taking steps to prevent the attrition of material. • Identify and assess the nature/scope of the scene, liaise with others present to identify actions already taken. Take immediate steps to preserve the scene for forensic examination, minimise the risk of cross-contamination. Start a scene log, where necessary, ensure the continuity/integrity of the scene log if passed on. Gather additional information from identified victims and witnesses, prioritise and assess their individual needs. Deal with victims and witnesses in an ethical manner in accordance with diversity and human rights. Establish the potential impact of the investigation on the community and take appropriate action. • Task colleagues, keep appropriate personnel informed and call for additional resources, as necessary, to ensure continued scene preservation. • Provide support, including crime prevention advice to victims and witnesses, as required. Liaise with internal and external support agencies as necessary. • Reassess the material gathered, ensure that it is recorded and stored in the correct manner. Follow up immediate identified lines of enquiry. Conduct house-to-house enquiries. Where applicable, take appropriate action to identify and arrest/re-arrest suspects. Ensure that material generated by the suspect is gathered in the appropriate manner to prevent cross-contamination. Carry out any searches and identification procedures in accordance with policy and legislation, and evaluate the material gathered as to its impact on the investigation. • Ensure a correct and prompt disposal of the suspect after carrying out an evidential assessment. • Obtain all the information necessary to complete the related documentation. Interrogate intelligence and crime recording systems. Ensure that intelligence gathered is prioritised and passed to the appropriate person or department. Prepare and submit case files in compliance with legislation and the manual of guidance for file completion. • Enter details into the appropriate reporting system in accordance with the National Crime Recording Standards and the Data Protection Act. Ensure other appropriate records are completed. • Ensure any scene log is handed over/closed and relevant personnel are briefed/debriefed as appropriate. Ensure continuity of evidence. • Prepare and present evidence to courts and other hearings. • At each stage of the investigation fully document the decision-making process and the rationale behind those processes.

Core Responsibilities	Activity no.	Activities The role holder should effectively deliver these key requirements
Investigation	45	**Interview suspects** Interview suspects in accordance with the legislation and the *Practical Guide to Investigative Interviewing* 2004. Effective performance • Plan and prepare for the interview. Obtain all relevant information and review enquiries made prior to the interview. Research intelligence systems. Identify any significant statements or unsolicited comments that have been made. • Identify category of interview. • Consult with legal representatives and manage the pre-interview briefing. Disclose material in accordance with the Criminal Justice and Public Order Act 1994. Make a written record of what was revealed and the process of revelation. Consider written briefings where phased revelation of information is planned and points to prove. • Conduct interview in accordance with codes of practice and the *Practical Guide to Investigative Interviewing* 2004. Record interview on tape, unless equipment is unavailable. Ensure the security/welfare of all persons present. Properly introduce exhibits during interview. Cover possible defences and points to prove. • Deal with contingencies in accordance with the current codes of practice and the *Practical Guide to Investigative Interviewing* 2004. • Conclude interview and process interview record. Endorse written interview record. Before you charge check with CPS if required. • Evaluate the information obtained during the interview and its impact on the investigation. Establish whether offence(s) have been proved. Update the officer in the case, as appropriate. Evaluate own performance against the *Practical Guide to Investigative Interviewing* 2004.
	46	**Interview victims and witnesses** Interview victims and witnesses in accordance with the law and with reference to the Victims Charter and the *Practical Guide to Investigative Interviewing* 2004. Effective performance • Plan and prepare for the interview in accordance with the *Practical Guide to Investigative Interviewing* 2004. • Research intelligence systems. Identify category of interviewee. Identify the interviewee's needs and provide appropriate support. Explain the purpose/format of the interview and the interviewee's legal entitlements. Explain to victims and witnesses relevant details of their involvement in the judicial process. • Conduct the interview assisting and enabling interviewees to recall their version of events, explore the information gained. Record interviewee's account of events, bearing in mind that should the interviewee become a suspect at a later date, the account will need to be treated as a 'significant statement'. • Write statements in a legible format and which contains all the information/evidence including full details of loss or injury and signature. Ensure the security/welfare of all persons present at the interview. Conclude interview and explain the legal process.

Core Responsibilities	Activity no.	Activities The role holder should effectively deliver these key requirements
Investigation	46 ●	**Interview victims and witnesses** Evaluate the information obtained during the interview and establish whether any offence(s) have been identified and/or proved. Evaluate the impact of the information against what is already known in the investigation and bring it to the attention of the officer in the case where appropriate. Evaluate own performance against the *Practical Guide to Investigative Interviewing* 2004.
	74	**Provide care for victims and witnesses** Ensure that the necessary care for victims and witnesses is provided in an ethical and empathic manner and in accordance with the legislation, policies and procedures. Effective performance ● Respond to complaints of crime as promptly as practicable. Identify the type of victim/witness and assess the impact on them taking appropriate action to meet their immediate needs. ● Establish and maintain a sensitive, supportive and appropriate relationship with victims/witnesses. Explain the police and external support services available to them and facilitate their referral, as required. Provide advice, guidance assistance and support that is ethical and relevant to the needs of the victim and witnesses in accordance with the legislation and policy. ● Give basic health and safety advice. Give basic crime prevention advice if appropriate. Provide a copy of 'Making a Victim Personal Statement'. Where appropriate, give, and/or arrange, advice regarding compensation. Explain to victims/witnesses the benefits and pitfalls of using the media in crime investigations. ● Where appropriate, arrange for specialist support intervention, e.g. alarm installation. Act as, or provide a reference point for future enquiries/additional information. Ensure that victim and witnesses are kept up to date with information and developments, provide appropriate assistance regarding their court appearance. ● Ensure care responsibilities are appropriately concluded. Record all actions and decisions as required.
	52	**Search persons or personal property** Search individuals or personal property in accordance with the relevant legislation, policy, procedures, whilst respecting the dignity of the individual and being aware of the possible impact on the community. Effective performance ● Ensure that you have the grounds and legal authority to carry out the search. Identify the possible risks involved, obtain support as required and inform appropriate personnel of your status. ● Inform person of the reason for the search and their rights in accordance with legislation. Keep the person informed of your actions. ● Using approved search techniques conduct a thorough search, as far as necessary, whilst having regard for the person's human rights and ensuring the health and safety of all concerned. Act in accordance with legislation.

Core Responsibilities	Activity no.	Activities The role holder should effectively deliver these key requirements
Investigation	52	**Search persons or personal property** • Seize any evidence found and ensure that cross-contamination is avoided and the exhibits are recovered, packaged and stored in accordance with current legislation and policies. Inform person about the result of the search. • Complete necessary documentation. • Search the vehicle used to transport prisoners for discarded items and or weapons. • Record evidence of search and submit it for supervision and intelligence.
	53	**Search vehicles, premises and land** Conduct search procedures using the best practice techniques in accordance with the relevant legislation and policy, whilst having regard for the health, safety and human rights. Effective performance • Liaise with appropriate departments and carry out required checks prior to search. Apply for and obtain the necessary verbal and written authorities/warrants. Plan the search taking into consideration the objective of the search, risk assessment, resource requirements and contingencies. • Brief and task personnel assisting in search using IIRMAC guidelines. • Exercise powers to search premises and/or execute search warrant. • Enter only using as much force as is necessary in the circumstances and having regard for the health and safety of all concerned. Provide owner/occupier with search documentation as required by law. • Carry out a systematic search safely and, as far as necessary, with due regard for the property and human rights of the owner/occupier(s). Where evidence is relevant ensure that cross-contamination is avoided and that exhibits are recovered, packaged and stored in accordance with current legislation and policies. • Search the vehicle used to transport prisoners for discarded items of evidence and or weapons. • Maintain communications with colleagues and update OIC/supervisor of any developments. Record details of search in accordance with legislation and policy. Leave the premises secure after search. • Report any damage to property and complete search documentation as required. Debrief other personnel involved in search and input information back into the intelligence system.

National Occupational Standards	
2G2 – Conduct investigations	2H1 – Interview victims and witnesses
2H2 – Interview suspects	2I1 – Search individuals
2I2 – Search vehicles, premises and land	1B9 – Provide initial support to individuals affected by offending or anti-social behaviour and assess their needs for further support

Core Responsibilities	Activity no.	Activities The role holder should effectively deliver these key requirements
Custody and prosecution	41	**Complete prosecution procedures** Complete prosecution procedures in accordance with codes of practice and relevant legislation. Effective performance • Where offender is not in custody, carry out appropriate prosecution procedures. • Ensure the immediate release of the person detained if insufficient evidence to prosecute and no further action is to be taken. Inform person detained that no further action will be taken. • Where offender is in custody and it becomes apparent that there is insufficient evidence to prosecute and no further action is anticipated ensure the immediate release of the person and inform them that no further action is to be taken. • Where offender is in custody and further enquiries need to be made, ensure person is released on bail as soon as appropriate. Ensure further enquiries are carried out thoroughly and expeditiously and that persons returning on bail are dealt with promptly. • Liaise with the relevant CPS office as early as possible in respect of any issues arising. • Where there is sufficient evidence to prosecute, review case disposal options taking into consideration the nature of the case, Home Office guidelines and antecedents. Inform Custody Officer of case disposal and bail recommendation. • Accurately complete all required identification and antecedents documentation and procedures. Update all relevant crime records. • Update all victims and witnesses as to the current situation regarding the investigation. • Consider victim personal statement.
	36	**Conduct custody reception procedures (arresting officer)** Attend the custody suite, as the arresting officer with the person detained under escort. Whilst ensuring the security and welfare of the person detained, comply with the custody reception procedures required by law, current codes of practice and policy. Effective performance • Maintain the health, safety and security of the person detained and persons present in the custody suite. • Explain to the Custody Officer the facts of arrest to prove compliance with the relevant law and current codes of practice. Inform the Custody Officer of any special arrest circumstances, such as restraint techniques used, illness/injuries warning signals and premises searched. • Ensure personal details and previous history checks of person detained are completed and Custody Officer informed. • Carry out search of person detained as required by Custody Officer and in accordance with the best practice techniques, legislation and policy. Deal with property as required by the Custody Officer. • Inform Custody Officer of any restrictions to rights and entitlements in accordance with codes of practice. Inform Custody Officer of the need for any forensic examination and/or identification procedures. Identify, record, handle and store exhibits in accordance with the legislation and policy. • Record any significant statements and unsolicited comments and other relevant information (i.e. medication).

Core Responsibilities	Activity no.	Activities The role holder should effectively deliver these key requirements
Custody and prosecution	35	**Conduct lawful arrest and process procedures** Carry out lawful arrest/process procedures in accordance with the relevant legal requirements and policy, having regard for human rights, security, health and safety of person(s) detained, members of the public, colleagues and self. Effective performance • Assess the initial allegation(s) to identify what offence has been committed. • Complete a thorough investigation where appropriate prior to arrest/process, ensure the identification of the suspect(s) is carried out in accordance with the PACE, case law and current codes of practice. • Make lawful arrest(s) or assist in making a lawful arrest(s) and re-arrest(s) when necessary in accordance with the relevant legislation and the current codes of practice. Correctly administer the caution. Comply with specified warrant/injunction conditions. • Treat the suspect as a crime scene. Apply arrest techniques in accordance with training and with consideration for the safety and security of self and others. Identify and take action to preserve forensic evidence. • Record and deal appropriately with any significant statement or unsolicited comments. • Search the vehicle used to transport prisoners for discarded items or evidence and or weapons. • Provide a safe and secure escort. Question person(s) only in accordance with current codes and practice. • Ensure that summons procedures and other disposal options are fully complied with as necessary. • Accurately record evidence of arrest/ process procedures as soon as practicable.
	42	**Prepare and present case files** Identify and present case materials, working with the Crown Prosecution Service or other relevant agencies/organisations to progress the case. Effective performance • Distinguish between evidence and unused material, identifying material that might undermine the prosecution or assist the defence. • Assimilate relevant detail from case papers. Ensure appropriate availability of all exhibits/disclosure material that will be relied upon in court. • Record, retain and reveal all unused material, distinguishing between sensitive and non-sensitive. • Ensure quality and accuracy of file contents, presenting evidence logically, with honesty and within required timescales. • Present honest and objective comments regarding the strengths and weaknesses of the case in a fair and justifiable manner to the CPS. • Liaise with the Criminal Justice Unit and/or Crown Prosecution Service or relevant agency for advice. As required submit the correct and completed case file to the Criminal Justice Units in the required time scales. Respond promptly and positively to any requests in respect of further actions.

147

Core Responsibilities	Activity no.	Activities The role holder should effectively deliver these key requirements
Custody and prosecution	44	**Present evidence in court and at other hearings** Attend court and give evidence in accordance with legislation. Effective performance • Respond to court warnings in accordance with instructions and legislation. • Ensure that you are fully prepared to give evidence at the allotted time and place. • Ensure availability, labelling, continuity and integrity of exhibits, if applicable. • Present verbal evidence to the court in a clear, confident and ethical manner and in accordance with the legislation and court procedures.

National Occupational Standards	
2G4 – Finalise investigations	2C3 – Arrest, detain and report individuals
2K2 – Present detained persons to custody	2K1 – Escort detained persons
2J1 – Prepare and submit case files	2J2 – Present evidence at court and other hearings

Core Responsibilities	Activity no.	Activities
Personal responsibility	206	**Comply with health and safety legislation** Ensure that you show a duty of care and take appropriate action to comply with health and safety requirements at all times. Effective performance • Ensure that you are in possession of the necessary health and safety equipment to carry out your role. • Organise your own work area to minimise risks to yourself and others. • Identify risks and hazards, taking prompt and appropriate action to deal with them in accordance with the relevant law and policy. • Operate and take care of all equipment in accordance with manufacturer instructions. • Utilise the appropriate safety techniques and ensure your actions conform to the law, policies and procedures, and training received. • Ensure you show a duty of care and support to yourself, others, taking the appropriate action to prevent and reduce health and safety risks. When incidents concerning health and safety occur, ensure that the appropriate support and medical assistance is provided when necessary. • Report and record all notifiable incidents/hazards accurately.
	660	**Maintain standards for security of information** Maintain personal responsibility for gathering, recording, storing, accessing and sharing of information in compliance with information security policy, procedures and codes of practice and legislation. Effective performance • Ensure that your level of knowledge and understanding of organisational policy, procedures, codes of practice and legislation relating to information security is maintained. • Ensure that all information gathered is accurate, sufficient and relevant to the purpose for which it is needed. • Access only systems or records of information to which you have authority and for an authorised purpose.

Core Responsibilities	Activity no.	Activities The role holder should effectively deliver these key requirements
Personal responsibility		• Record and store the information gathered in accordance with organisational policy, procedure, codes of practice and legislation. • Ensure the information you gather and record is maintained in the authorised format and disseminated to authorised personnel only. • Ensure that information shared with internal/external is appropriate and sufficient for their needs and is done so in a timely manner in compliance with policy, procedure, codes of practice and legislation. • Inform relevant people of any possible improvements to systems and procedures to enhance information security. • Inform relevant people of any breaches of policy, procedures, codes of practice or legislation in respect of information security.
	217	**Maintain standards of professional practice** Ensure your behaviour complies with organisational values and organise your own work effectively to meet the demands of your role. Identify, implement and monitor development activities to enhance your own performance. Effective performance • Act at all times in accordance with organisational values. As necessary conform to relevant codes of practice. • Ensure that you understand the objectives and priorities relevant to your role. • Plan activities that are consistent with your objectives. Set demanding goals for yourself. • Regularly review performance against your objectives, making adjustments as necessary to help you achieve your plans. • Assess your skills and identify personal development needs at regular intervals. Undertake continuous self-development activities. Keep yourself up to date with changes affecting your role. • Obtain feedback from relevant people and use it to enhance your performance. Contribute positively to performance reviews with relevant individuals.
	141	**Promote equality, diversity and human rights in working practices** Promote equality, diversity and human rights in working practices by developing and maintaining positive working relationships, ensuring that colleagues are treated fairly and contributing to developing equality of opportunity in working practices. Effective performance • Develop and maintain positive relationships with colleagues, regardless of their culture, religion, ethnicity, sex, marital status, sexual orientation and any disability. Ensure that you are approachable and that your conduct towards colleagues is open and honest. Deal with differences in opinion in a manner that will avoid offence. • Contribute to developing and maintaining equality of opportunity in working practices by complying with legislation and organisational policies. Advise colleagues about equal opportunity policies and procedures. • Ensure that colleagues are treated fairly. Behave in a non-discriminatory way and challenge the discriminatory behaviour of others. Be supportive of colleagues who wish to raise issues about discriminatory practice.

Core Responsibilities	Activity no.	Activities The role holder should effectively deliver these key requirements
Personal responsibility	127	**Provide an organisational response recognising the needs of all communities** Build and maintain community relations by providing a service that is responsive to the needs of all communities and by ensuring that those affected by crime receive a fair and anti-discriminatory service. Effective performance • Develop effective working relationships with members of all communities within your local area in order that their issues and concerns can be voiced. Communicate effectively with community groups and key community members, acknowledging and respecting differences. Consult with communities to identify issues and concerns. • Take consistent action to deliver solutions to the issues and concerns of communities. Help produce, implement, and monitor and evaluate initiatives which provide solutions to the issues and problems that have been identified. Help community members to realise their own capacity for preventing crime and support them in developing this. • Respond effectively to hate crime. Respond promptly and sympathetically to victims of racist incidents, keep them regularly informed on case developments. Collect, record and report intelligence about hate crime with other partners (i.e. statutory partners, social services). • Deliver a fair and anti-discriminatory service to all those involved in enquiries. Encourage the reporting of crime by all communities. Ensure that when using your discretion you are not influenced by stereotyping or other forms of discrimination.

National Occupational Standards		
4G2 – Ensure your own actions reduce the risks to health and safety		1A2 – Communicate effectively with members of communities
1A4 – Foster people's equality, diversity and rights		1A1 – Use police actions in a fair and justified way
4C1 – Develop one's own knowledge and practice		

Core Responsibilities	Activity no.	Activities
Health and safety	207	**Provide first aid** Identify the nature of illness or injury and provide the necessary first aid treatment in accordance with approved procedures. Effective performance • Assess the situation quickly and calmly, identifying the nature of the illness or injury. Identify risks to yourself, casualty and others present. Take immediate action to protect the casualty, you and others present from ongoing risks. • Decide priorities of treatment, dealing with life-threatening conditions first. When there is more than one casualty decide who needs treatment most urgently. • Call for assistance or request specialist help as soon as the casualty's condition indicates such action is necessary. • Administer treatment appropriate to the needs of the casualty. Administer CPR promptly and effectively, as required. Use first aid equipment in accordance with instructions. Wear appropriate protective equipment.

Core Responsibilities	Activity no.	Activities The role holder should effectively deliver these key requirements
Health and safety		• Maintain records and provide accurate information to medical personnel, as required. • Clean up after dealing with a casualty as soon as possible. Dispose of materials used to administer first aid. Replenish the first aid kit.
National Occupational Standards		
4G4 – Administer first aid		

Behaviour Area	Level	Behaviour Description
Working with others		**Respect for race and diversity** Considers and shows respect for the opinions, circumstances and feelings of colleagues and members of the public, no matter what their race, religion, position, background, circumstances, status or appearance.
	A	Shows understanding for other people's views and takes them into account. Is tactful and diplomatic when dealing with people, treating them with dignity and respect at all times. Understands and is sensitive to social, cultural and racial differences. Positive indicators Sees issue from other people's viewpoints. Is polite, tolerant and patient when dealing with people, treating them with respect and dignity. Respects the needs of everyone involved when sorting out disagreements. Shows understanding and sensitivity to people's problems, vulnerabilities and needs. Deals with diversity issues and gives positive practical support to staff whom may feel vulnerable. Makes people feel valued by listening to and supporting their needs and interests. Uses language in an appropriate way and is sensitive to the way it may affect people. Identifies and respects other people's values within the law. Acknowledges and respects a broad range of social and cultural customs and beliefs. Understands what offends others and adapts own actions accordingly. Respects confidentiality, wherever appropriate. Delivers difficult messages. Challenges attitudes and behaviour that are abusive, aggressive and discriminatory.
		Team working Develops strong working relationships inside and outside the team to achieve common goals. Breaks down barriers between groups and involves others in discussions and decisions.
	C	Shows that they can work effectively as a team member and helps build relationships within it. Actively helps and supports others to achieve team goals. Positive indicators Understands own role in a team. Actively takes part in team tasks in the workplace. Is open and approachable. Makes time to get to know people. Co-operates with and supports others. Offers to help other people. Asks for and accepts help when needed. Develops mutual trust and confidence in others. Willingly takes on unpopular or routine tasks. Contributes to team objectives no matter what the direct personal benefit may be. Acknowledges that there is often a need to be a member of more than one team.

Behaviour Area	Level	Behaviour Description
Working with others		**Community and customer focus** Focuses on the customer and provides a high-quality service that is tailored to meet their individual needs. Understands the communities that are served and shows an active commitment to policing that reflects their needs and concerns.
	C	Shows they can provide a high level of service to customers. Maintain contact with customers, works out what they need and responds to them. Positive indicators Presents an appropriate image to the public and other organisations. Supports strategies that aim to build an organisation that reflects the community it serves. Focuses on the customer in all activities. Tries to sort out customers' problems as quickly as possible. Apologises for mistakes and sorts them out as quickly as possible. Responds quickly to customer requests. Makes sure that customers are satisfied with the service they receive. Manages customer expectations. Keeps customers updated on progress. Balances customer needs with organisational needs.
		Effective communication Communicates ideas and information effectively, both verbally and in writing. Uses language and a style of communication that is appropriate to the situation and people being addressed. Makes sure that others understand what is going on.
	B	Shows they can speak clearly and concisely, and do not use jargon. Uses plain English and correct grammar. Listens carefully to understand. Positive indicators Deals with issues directly Clearly communicates needs and instructions. Clearly communicates decisions and the reasons behind them. Communicates face to face wherever possible and if it is appropriate. Speaks with authority and confidence. Changes the style of communication to meet the needs of the audience. Manages group discussions effectively. Summarises information to check people understand it. Supports arguments and recommendations effectively in writing. Produces well-structured reports and written summaries.
		Problem-solving Gathers information from a range of sources. Analyses information to identify problems and issues, and makes effective decisions.
	C	Gathers enough relevant information to understand specific issues and events. Uses information to identify problems and draw logical conclusions. Makes a good decision. Positive indicators Identifies where to get information and gets it. Gets as much information as is appropriate on all aspects of a problem. Separates relevant information from irrelevant information, and important information from unimportant information.

Behaviour Area	Level	Behaviour Description
Working with others	C	Takes in information quickly and accurately. Reviews all the information gathered to understand the situation and draw logical conclusions. Identifies and links causes and effects. Identifies what can and cannot be changed. Takes a systematic approach to solving problems. Remains impartial and avoids jumping to conclusions. Refers to procedures and precedents, as necessary, before making decisions. Makes good decisions that take account of all relevant factors.
Achieving results		**Personal responsibility** Takes personal responsibility for making things happen and achieving results. Displays motivation, commitment, perseverance and conscientiousness. Acts with a high degree of integrity.
	B	Shows they can take personal responsibility for own actions and for sorting out issues or problems that arise. Is focused on achieving results to required standards and developing skills and knowledge. Positive indicators Takes personal responsibility for own actions. Takes on tasks without having to be asked. Uses initiative. Takes action to resolve problems and fulfil own responsibilities. Keeps promises and does not let colleagues down. Takes pride in own work. Is conscientious in completing work on time. Follows things through to a satisfactory conclusion. Shows enthusiasm about own role. Focuses on a task even if it is routine. Improves own job-related knowledge and keeps it up to date. Is open, honest and genuine, standing up for what is right.
		Resilience Shows resilience even in difficult circumstances. Prepared to make difficult decisions and has the confidence to see them through.
	A	Shows they have confidence to perform own role without unnecessary support in normal circumstances. Acts in appropriate way and controls emotions. Positive indicators Is reliable in a crisis, remains calm and thinks clearly. Sorts out conflict and deals with hostility and provocation in a calm and restrained way. Responds to challenges rationally, avoiding inappropriate emotion. Deals with difficult emotional issues and then moves on. Manages conflicting pressures and tensions. Maintains professional ethics when confronted with pressure from others. Copes with ambiguity and deals with uncertainty and frustration. Resists pressure to make quick decisions where full consideration is needed. Remains focused and in control of situations. Makes and carries through decisions, even if they are unpopular, difficult or controversial. Stands firmly by a position when it is right to do so.

Appendix 2
Legislation

Theft

Theft Act 1968

1. (1) A person is guilty of theft if he dishonestly appropriates property belonging to another with the intention of permanently depriving the other of it ...

Burglary

Theft Act 1968

9. (1) A person is guilty of burglary if—

(a) he enters any building or part of a building as a trespasser and with intent to commit any such offence as is mentioned in subsection (2) below; or

(b) having entered any building or part of a building as a trespasser he steals or attempts to steal anything in the building or that part of it or attempts to inflict on any person therein any grievous bodily harm.

(2) The offences referred to in subsection (1)(a) above are offences of stealing anything in the building or part of a building in question, of inflicting on any person therein any grievous bodily harm, and of doing unlawful damage to the building or anything therein.

Power of arrest

Police and Criminal Evidence Act 1984 (as amended by Senior Organised Crime and Police Act 2005)

24. (1) A constable may arrest without a warrant—

(a) anyone who is about to commit an offence;

(b) anyone who is in the act of committing an offence;

(c) anyone whom he has reasonable grounds for suspecting to be about to commit an offence;

(d) anyone whom he has reasonable grounds for suspecting to be committing an offence.

(2) If a constable has reasonable grounds for suspecting that an offence has been committed, he may arrest without a warrant anyone whom he has reasonable grounds to suspect of being guilty of it.

(3) If an offence has been committed, a constable may arrest without a warrant—
(a) anyone who is guilty of the offence;
(b) anyone whom he has reasonable grounds for suspecting to be guilty of it.

(4) But the power of summary arrest conferred by subsection (1), (2) or (3) is exercisable only if the constable has reasonable grounds for believing that for any of the reasons mentioned in subsection (5) it is necessary to arrest the person in question.

(5) The reasons are—
(a) to enable the name of the person in question to be ascertained (in the case where the constable does not know, and cannot readily ascertain, the person's name, or has reasonable grounds for doubting whether a name given by the person as his name is his real name);
(b) correspondingly as regards the person's address;
(c) to prevent the person in question—
(i) causing physical injury to himself or any other person;
(ii) suffering physical injury;
(iii) causing loss of or damage to property;
(iv) committing an offence against public decency (subject to subsection (6)); or
(v) causing an unlawful obstruction of the highway;
(d) to protect a child or other vulnerable person from the person in question;
(e) to allow the prompt and effective investigation of the offence or of the conduct of the person in question;
(f) to prevent any prosecution for the offence from being hindered by the disappearance of the person in question.

(6) Subsection (5)(c)(iv) applies only where members of the public going about their normal business cannot reasonably be expected to avoid the person in question.

Search and seizure

Police and Criminal Evidence Act 1984 (as amended by the Senior Organised Crime and Police Act 2005)

17. (1) A constable may enter and search any premises for the purpose—

  (a) of executing—

    (i) a warrant of arrest issued in connection with or arising out of criminal proceedings, or

    (ii) a warrant of commitment issued under section 76 of the Magistrates' Courts Act 1980;

  (b) of arresting a person for an indictable offence;

  (c) of arresting a person for an offence under—

    (i) section 1 (prohibition of uniforms in connection with political objects) ... of the Public Order Act 1936;

    (ii) any enactment contained in section 6 to 8 or 10 of the Criminal Law Act 1977 (offences relating to entering and remaining on property);

    (iii) section 4 of the Public Order Act 1986 (fear or provocation of violence);

    (iiia) section 4 (driving, etc. when under influence of drink or drugs) or 163 (failure to stop when required to do so by a constable in uniform) of the Road Traffic Act 1988;

    (iv) section 76 of the Criminal Justice and Public Order Act 1994 (failure to comply with an interim possession order);

  (ca) of arresting, in pursuance of section 32(1A) of the Children and Young Persons Act 1969, any child or young person who has been remanded or committed to local authority accommodation under section 23(1) of that Act;

  (cb) of recapturing any person who is, or is deemed for any purpose to be, unlawfully at large while liable to be detained—

    (i) in a prison, remand centre, young offender institution or secure training centre; or

    (ii) in pursuance of section 92 of the Powers of Criminal Courts (Sentencing) Act 2000 (dealing with children and young persons guilty of grave crimes) in any other place;

  (d) of recapturing any person whatever who is unlawfully at large and whom he is pursuing; or

  (e) of saving life or limb or preventing serious damage to property.

18. (1) A constable may enter and search any premises occupied or controlled by a person who is under arrest for an indictable offence, if he has reasonable grounds for suspecting that there is on the premises evidence, other than items subject to legal privilege, that relates—
   (a) to that offence; or
   (b) to some other indictable offence which is connected with or similar to that offence.

  (2) A constable may seize and retain anything for which he may search under subsection (1) above.

  (3) The power to search conferred by subsection (1) above is only a power to search to the extent that is reasonably required for the purpose of discovering such evidence.

  (4) Subject to subsection (5) below, the powers conferred by this section may not be exercised unless an officer of the rank of inspector or above has authorised them in writing.

  (5) A constable may conduct a search under subsection (1)—
   (a) before the person is taken to a police station or released on bail under section 30A, and
   (b) without obtaining an authorisation under subsection (4), if the condition in subsection (5A) is satisfied.

(5A) The condition is that the presence of the person at a place (other than a police station) is necessary for the effective investigation of the offence.

  (6) If a constable conducts a search by virtue of subsection (5) above, he shall inform an officer of the rank of inspector or above that he has made the search as soon as practicable after he has made it.

  (7) An officer who—
   (a) authorises a search; or
   (b) is informed of a search under subsection (6) above, shall make a record in writing—
      (i) of the grounds for the search; and
      (ii) of the nature of the evidence that was sought.

  (8) If the person who was in occupation or control of the premises at the time of the search is in police detention at the time the record is to be made, the officer shall make the record as part of his custody record.

32. (1) A constable may search an arrested person, in any case where the person to be searched has been arrested at a place other than a police station, if the constable has reasonable grounds for believing that the arrested person may present a danger to himself or others.

  (2) Subject to subsections (3) to (5) below, a constable shall also have power in any such case:

(a) to search the arrested person for anything—
   (i) which he might use to assist him to escape from lawful custody; or
   (ii) which might be evidence relating to an offence; and
(b) if the offence for which he has been arrested is an indictable offence, to enter and search any premises in which he was when arrested or immediately before he was arrested for evidence relating to the offence.

(3) The power to search conferred by subsection (2) above is only a power to search to the extent that is reasonably required for the purpose of discovering any such thing or any such evidence.

(4) The powers conferred by this section to search a person are not to be construed as authorising a constable to require a person to remove any of his clothing in public other than the outer coat, jacket or gloves but they do authorise a search of a person's mouth.

(5) A constable may not search a person in the exercise of the power conferred by subsection (2)(b) above unless he has reasonable grounds for believing that the person to be searched may have concealed on him anything for which a search is permitted under that paragraph.

Offence of leaving litter

Environmental Protection Act 1990

87. (1) If any person throws down, drops or otherwise deposits in, into or from any place to which this section applies, and leaves, any thing whatsoever in such circumstances as to cause, or contribute to, or tend to lead to, the defacement by litter of any place to which this section applies he shall, subject to subsection (2) below, be guilty of an offence.

(2) No offence is committed under this section where the depositing and leaving of the thing was—
   (a) authorised by law, or
   (b) done with the consent of the owner, occupier or other person or authority having control of the place in or into which that thing was deposited.

(3) ...

(4) In this section 'public open place' means a place in the open air to which the public are entitled or permitted to have access without payment; and any covered place open to the air on at least one side and available for public use shall be treated as a public open place.

Causing harassment, alarm or distress

Public Order Act 1986

5. (1)   A person is guilty of an offence if he:

   (a) uses threatening, abusive or insulting words or behaviour, or disorderly behaviour, or

   (b) displays any writing, sign or other visible representation which is threatening, abusive or insulting, within the hearing or sight of a person likely to be caused harassment, alarm or distress thereby.

(2)   An offence under this section may be committed in a public or a private place, except that no offence is committed where the words or behaviour are used or the writing, sign or other visible representation is displayed by a person inside a dwelling and the other person is also inside that or another dwelling.

(4)   A constable may arrest a person without warrant if—

   (a) he engages in offensive conduct which a constable warns him to stop, and

   (b) he engages in further offensive conduct immediately or shortly after the warning.

Assault occasioning actual bodily harm

Offences Against the Person Act 1861

47.   Whosoever shall be convicted upon an indictment of any assault occasioning actual bodily harm shall be liable ... to be imprisoned for any term not exceeding five years.

Definitions

Road Traffic Act 1988

185. (1)   In this Act—

   ...

   'motor vehicle' means ... a mechanically propelled vehicle intended or adapted for use on roads ...

192. (1)   In this Act—

   ...

   'road', in relation to England and Wales, means any highway and any other road to which the public has access, and includes bridges over which a road passes ...

Index

addresses, verification 55
ADVOKATE mnemonic 88, 110
alarm, causing 160
arrest
   court appearance 135
   power of 155–6
   and power to search 126
assault
   and battery 125
   occasioning actual bodily harm 125, 160

back-up request 50
bail, conditional 134
beat officers 57
breach of the peace 120–1
burglary
   arrest 111–13
   charge 114
   circumstances 104–5
   forensic investigation 108–9
   intelligence unit 110–11
   interview 113
   investigation 105–10
   legislation 155
   offence 102, 105
   scenario 102–4
   suspect 110–13
   victim support 105, 114

causing grievous bodily harm with
     intent 125
certificate of insurance 25–7, 37
   power to require production 41
children support, domestic violence 132–4
common assault/battery 125
community officers 59
computerised information 46–9, 110–11
conditional bail 135–6
CPO PLAN ID mnemonic 111
Criminal Justice Act 1988, s 39 125

description points 88
detention

authorisation 127–9
   and cultural differences 129
   detainee's rights 86
distress, causing 160
domestic homicide statistics 118
domestic violence
   arrest 125–7
      court appearance 135
      discretion 124
   children support 131–3
   communication centre 119, 120, 126
   conditional bail 134
   custody officer 127–9, 134–5
   definition 117
   details of assault 133
   detention 129
   domestic violence policy 133
   enhanced evidence gathering 130
   force policies 133
   incident log details 133
   incomplete 999 call 119–20
   investigation 121–3
   offences 125
   power to enter premises 121–2
   scenario 118–20
   section 47 assault 125, 135
   victim support 124, 132–4
   witness statement 131, 132
driving documents 19
   see also driving licence; provisional
      driving licence
   failure to produce 29–34
   personal safety 22
   pocket notebook entries 28–9, 34, 38
   power to require production 21, 40, 40–1
   scenarios 19–20, 29, 34–6
   statement of evidence 40
driving licence 22–3
   see also provisional driving licence
   offences 41

enhanced evidence gathering 130–1
Environmental Protection Act 1990, s 87(1)
     50, 54

file of evidence 135
force computerised information system 55
forensic investigation 106–9

golden hour, the 62
grievous bodily harm with intent 125

harassment 125, 160
HO/RT 1 form 30–4
homicide, domestic, statistics 118

identity
    description points 88
    verification 53–4
incident log details 134
insurance certificate *see* certificate of
        insurance
intelligence unit 110–11
interview
    see also PEACE model
    account/clarification and challenge
        97
    arrangements 95
    closure 97
    codes of practice 95, 97
    defences 94
    engage and explain 95–7
    evaluation 97
    facts, the 94–6
    legal representative, pre-interview
        disclosure 95
    nature of offence 113
    planning/preparation 93–9, 134
    suspect's intent 94

legislation 155–60
litter offences 49–50, 54

missing persons
    information
        assessed 64–7
        received 64
    interviews 71–2
    risk assessment 69–71
    scenario 63–71
    search 71
    useful information 63
MOT test certificate 27–8
    power to require production 41
motor vehicle, definition 71, 160

notebook entries 28–9, 34, 38–9

Offences Against the Person Act 1861, ss 86,
        108–9, 110, 125, 135

PEACE model 113, 134
    see also interview
personal safety 47
pocket notebook entries 28–9, 34, 38–40
        87–8,
Police and Criminal Evidence Act 1984
    codes of practice
    s 17(1)(b) 121
    s 17(1)(g) 121
    s 18 113
    s 24 124
    s 25 50–2
    s 32 50, 52, 54, 84, 126
Police National Computer (PNC) 46–7, 53–4,
        55, 83, 111
power
    of arrest 155–6
    of search 126
    to enter premises 121–2
    to require production, certificates of
        insurance/MOT test 41
Protection from Harassment Act 1997 125
provisional driving licence 24
    see also driving licence
    offences 36–40, 41
Public Order Act 1986, s 5 and (1) 50, 55

R v Turnball 88
reporting for summons 49
reprisals, fear 46, 48, 56
risk assessment 68–71
road, definition 160
Road Traffic Act 1988 25
    s 22 30
    s 87 41
    s 164 40
    s 165 41
    s 185(1) 21
Road Vehicles (Construction and Use)
        Regulations 1986, reg 103 41

search and seizure 157–9
Serious Organised Crime and Police Act 2005
        111
shoplifting

arrest 83–4
communications centre 80–1, 84
custody officer 85–6
definition 80
interview *see* interview
items of evidence 85
pocket notebook entry 86–7
scenario 80–1
store detective 81–2
suspect's
  details 82–3
  identification/description 88
  intent 94
witness statement 87–91
statement of evidence 40, 132

theft 82, 91–2, 155
Theft Act 1968
  s 1 105
    (1) 91–2
  s 9 102

unnecessary obstruction 20, 30
offence 41

vehicle
driver/ownership 20–1
insurance *see* certificate of insurance
road offences 20

victim support
burglary 105
domestic violence 131, 132–3, 135

witness statement 87–91
wounding, offence 125

youth disorder 44
addresses, verification 55
arrest 50–2
back-up request 50
charges 56
communications centre 45, 46–7,
  50, 55
complaint 45, 48, 56
custody officer 53–6
identity, verification 53–4
information received 45–6
initial approach 46–7
offences committed 39–40
paperwork 56
personal safety 47, 50
priority 45
reprisals, fear 46, 48, 56
scenario 44
subsequent actions 56